THE FAMILIES BOOK

True Stories about Real Kids and
the People They Live With and Love

Fun Things to Do with Your Family

Making Family Trees and Keeping Family Traditions

Solving Family Problems

Staying Close to Faraway Relatives

And More!

Arlene Erlbach

Photographs by Stephen J. Carrera
Edited by Pamela Espeland

free Spirit
PUBLISHING

Library of Congress Cataloging-in-Publication Data

Erlbach, Arlene
    The families book : true stories about real kids and the people they live with and love ... / Arlene Erlbach : photographs by Stephen J. Carrera : edited by Pamela Espeland.
        p.   cm.
    "Fun things to do with your family, making family trees and keeping family traditions, solving family problems, staying close to faraway relatives, and more!"
    Includes index.
    Summary: Discusses, using case studies, what strengthens and weakens family life and how relatives interact.
    ISBN 1-57542-002-3 (pbk. : alk. paper)
    1. Family—Case studies—Juvenile literature. 2. Children—Family relationships—Case studies—Juvenile literature. 3. Family recreation—Juvenile literature. [1. Family. 2. Interpersonal relations.] I. Espeland, Pamela. II. Carrera, Stephen J. III. Title.
HQ744.E74   1996
306.85—dc20

95-45623
CIP
AC

Cover and book design by MacLean & Tuminelly
Text illustrations by Lisa Wagner
Index compiled by Eileen Quam and Theresa Wolner

10   9   8   7   6   5   4   3   2   1

Printed in the United States of America

Free Spirit Publishing Inc.
400 First Avenue North, Suite 616
Minneapolis, MN 55401-1730
(612) 338-2068

DEDICATION

In memory of Patrick Brian McCoskey,
April 23, 1986—April 13, 1995.

ACKNOWLEDGMENTS

I would like to extend my warmest thanks to the following people for suggesting possible families for this project. Without their help, this book would not have been possible.

Elsa Alvarez
Dorota Bergman
Kathy Bostrum
Marlene Targ Brill
Steve Brown
Carol Dale
Carol Erlbach
Ilse Erlbach
Rhonda Fryman
Anne and Stanley Hollenbeck
Margaret Collino Lyzen
Jennie Montgomery
Susan Myers
Simone Poulos
Marge Venetico
Cely Weinstein

And I would like to thank Jan Welter of Children's Services at Lutheran General Hospital in Park Ridge, Illinois, and all of the families who participated and gave so generously of their time.

A.E.

CONTENTS

INTRODUCTION

MAYBE YOU LIVE with one of your parents. Maybe you live with both. Or maybe you share your home with a stepparent, your biological brothers and sisters, and the stepparent's children.

The people you live with are your *family*. You have good times together. You depend on each other when times are tough. Sometimes your family members annoy or aggravate you, but you still love each other. You probably spend more time with your family than with anyone else.

When I was growing up, most families had two parents, and most mothers did not work outside the home. People hardly ever got divorced, so blended families were rare. Children who were adopted, children whose parents were divorced, and children whose parents had different religious beliefs often felt uncomfortable talking about their situations.

Things have changed a lot since then. Kids today live in many different kinds of families—so many that it's impossible to say which kind is "typical." Each family is unique. More people feel free to talk about their families and enjoy them just the way they are.

In this book, you'll meet kids from many types of families. Some of the families may be similar to yours, but others will be very different. You'll discover what kids love about their families— and what makes them angry. You'll find out about some of the neat things they do together—and how kids deal with annoying family members. But most of all, you'll appreciate how important families are to you and to other young people.

I'd like to hear about you and your family (or families, since some kids have more than one). You can write to me at this address:

Arlene Erlbach
c/o Free Spirit Publishing Inc.
400 First Avenue North, Suite 616
Minneapolis, MN 55401-1730

I hope to hear from you.

Arlene Erlbach

FAMILIES

Randy and Aaron

AGE 11

Some families have stepsiblings and stepparents.

RANDY: I HAVE A STEPDAD, regular dad, mom, and a stepbrother named Aaron. Aaron is three weeks younger than I am, so I think of him as my younger brother. Of course, he's not a *little* brother. He's a brother my same age who happened to be born three weeks after I was born.

My mother got divorced when I was about three years old. I don't remember what it was like when my biological dad and mom lived together.

I've always known Aaron and his dad. Aaron's mother was my Aunt Phyllis's best friend. (Aunt Phyllis is my mom's sister.) Aaron's mom died when Aaron was three. About a year later, my mom started dating Aaron's father.

When my mom started dating Aaron's dad, I didn't think about it much. But when I heard that they were getting married and I'd have a brother, that seemed weird. I'd never had a brother before, so I didn't know what it would be like. I didn't know what it would be like having a stepdad either.

Sometimes I hate having a stepbrother. Other times I like it.

I guess I feel pretty much about Aaron how other kids feel about their biological brothers and sisters.

Even though Aaron has his own friends, he likes to tag along when I do things with my friends. That would be okay, but Aaron doesn't always like to do the stuff we want to do when we want to do it. Like once we went to

Clockwise from top: STEVEN (AARON'S DAD, RANDY'S STEPDAD), AARON, SHARON (MOM) HOLDING ARNIE THE DOG, RANDY

the mall and all of us were supposed to go home together. Aaron didn't want to leave. He wanted to play at the video arcade. We left without him and my mom got mad at both of us. But that's how Aaron is. He wants to do what he wants to do. He's not big on going along with the group's decision.

Aaron can be very helpful. He's good at math and helps me with it. I'm not as good at math as he is. I'm a better reader, though. Aaron is better at helping out around the house and keeping his room neat. My mom says we're complete opposites, and she's right about that.

My stepdad and my real dad are complete opposites, too. My real dad likes to play sports with me, like baseball and basketball. I see him on Tuesdays and every other weekend. He yells when he gets mad. My stepdad is quiet and never yells at me or Aaron. He's a psychologist. I can talk to him about things I may not want to discuss with other people. He's a very understanding type of adult.

Having a stepbrother means sharing things with each other, but that's not bad. Actually, it's good. For Hanukkah, both Aaron and I got money. I bought a Sega with my money. Aaron bought a TV, which he keeps in his room. Most every night I watch it with him. He can play with my Sega whenever he wants, and I can watch his TV anytime. I like that kind of sharing. Since we watch TV together so much, I usually end up sleeping in Aaron's room.

Sometimes, if my mom or dad gets mad at either of us, the punishment is we have to sleep in our own rooms. I'd rather be with Aaron than alone. So if I really think about it, I like having a stepbrother.

AARON: I USUALLY LIKE having a stepbrother. Randy has his group of friends, and I have my group of friends. So having a stepbrother gives me a chance to know lots of different people. I like it when all of us play Sega and basketball together.

I like it at night when Randy and I watch TV together, too. Our favorites are "The Simpsons" and sports. It's fun to watch programs and have somebody my age to talk about them with.

Sometimes Randy makes me mad. He'll make funny noises to aggravate people. Sometimes it's funny. At other times it makes me mad, like when I'm watching TV, reading, or doing my homework. Randy doesn't always stop when I want him to. He just keeps on going. Then I tell our mom and she tells him to stop. Randy may stop the noises for a while. Then he'll start making them again.

Our mom is pretty fair about getting mad at us. When we get too noisy or silly, we get on her nerves. So we both get punished. Then we have to go to our separate rooms and play quietly. When we don't do our chores around the house, both our allowances get docked.

I have a feeling my real mom would have gotten madder at me when I didn't do chores or acted silly and noisy. Still, I wish I could still be with her. But I usually feel fortunate to have my stepmom for a stepmother.

My stepmom can be really nice. She'll take me and Randy places, like the movies or the mall. She's a good cook. She makes things to eat, like pizza and spaghetti.

Randy is close to my dad, but I don't mind sharing him. Every morning at 6:30, my dad and I have breakfast together alone. We talk privately. My dad teaches me things, like how to do algebra.

I don't really know Randy's dad very well. I don't see him, since Randy goes to visit him. He doesn't come here. When Randy's gone on Saturdays, I don't miss him that much. I'm in a bowling league on Saturdays. Afterwards I'll play with my own friends, read, or play Sega alone. Then when Randy comes back we watch TV with each other and play Sega.

I guess it's good that we have a regular break from each other. We have some time away from each other—and the house is quieter.

Katrina

Age 14

Some families have parents who are divorced.

KATRINA: I GUESS YOU COULD SAY that right now I'm a daddy's girl. I've lived with my dad ever since I was seven years old. My parents have been divorced since I was four years old. At first my parents had joint custody, so I lived with my mom during the week. On weekends I'd stay with my dad from Friday until Sunday night. After a while, my mom and I moved to Louisiana. Two years after that, I decided I wanted to live with my dad. So my parents decided that he would have custody and I'd live with him. Living with my dad meant I had to move to Chicago. So when I was seven, two important changes happened in my life.

Even though I enjoy living with my dad, not a day goes by that I don't think about my mom. My mom and I talk and write, but it's not the same as living with her.

My dad is a very special person. He takes me to restaurants or to the theater about twice a month. Our favorite restaurants are Greek Islands, Eduardo's (an Italian restaurant), and Hamburger Hamlet. Recently we went to a play called *Tony 'n' Tina's Wedding*. That was awesome. The play was about two people getting married, but the audience took part in the play, too. So the experience was like going to a wedding and watching a play. We even ate the wedding dinner and danced, just like we would have at a real wedding.

My father is very handsome. That's not just because I say so. Other people think he's handsome, too. He even models for a hair goods company. I'm proud to be seen with my dad, so when we go out, I dress up in good jeans or a skirt.

My dad spends lots of time talking with me. We talk about school and the news. He's a very knowledgeable man. He's the marketing director of a large dairy production company. He has a philosophy that I try to live by: "Be a leader, not a follower."

Sometimes my father cooks, and sometimes I do. I'm good at making hamburgers. My dad's devised a dish that he calls his stew. It's a mixture of sausage, broccoli, corn, and whatever other vegetables he throws in. I think his stew is okay—but he's very proud

KATRINA AND HER DAD, KARRIEM

of it. I guess I'd rather have a hamburger than my dad's stew. But I don't tell my dad that. I'd probably hurt his feelings.

Even though I don't live with a woman, I do have women in my life. I'm especially close to my Aunt Grethel and Aunt Lynne. They give me advice on boys and clothes. I also have a boy cousin a year older than me, and I talk to him a lot, too. I have conversations with him about boy-and-girl relationships. I see my aunt and cousins about every other week, so I'm very close to them.

In a few weeks, I'll be graduating from eighth grade. My mom is sending me a dress. Of course, she'll be there. I won't pretend that my mom and dad will get back together, like some kids would. I wouldn't even want that. My mom and dad don't get along. So things are best the way they are. I'm grateful that I have two parents and a close relationship with each of them.

D.C., Sean, and Dusty

AGES 14, 12, AND 8

Some families work together and share responsibilities.

D.C.: WE LIVE ON A FARM. I like it, but living on a farm means having responsibilities, like helping with gardening and the animals. There are always fun things to do, too. My brothers and I can swim, raft, and fish on our farm. A pond goes right through our land. We have lots of pets—six collies* and six cats.

Where I live, homes are located far from each other. So I can't walk over to a friend's to play or hang out. I play with my brothers Sean and Dusty a lot. The times I do have friends over, Dusty wants to join us. He'll do really embarrassing things, like sing a song to be cool and then use the wrong words.

My family is very diplomatic. On important things, we take a vote. Like if we're going on vacation, every member votes on when, if, and where. If we're going out to eat, we'll vote on that, too. That way, everyone gets a fair chance to do what they want to do.

---

* The collies are Lisa, 4; Moe, 1 1/2; Lucy, 1; Oxie, 2; Nicki, 3; and Boon, 4 months.

Left to right: TWO OF THE COLLIES, DUSTY, SEAN, D.C.

Our family also runs businesses together. My brother Sean and I collect baseball cards and sell them at flea markets. We might buy a big box of 800 cards. Then we'll resell them. But first Sean and I go through the box together. We decide very equally who gets which cards to sell.

My family also breeds collies. We have about three litters a year. Each of us helps take care of the pups after they're born. Then each of my brothers and I choose a puppy and sell it. They go for three to four hundred dollars each. My parents put the dog money in a college savings account for us.

The puppy business isn't as profitable as it sounds. Sometimes it's hard to breed puppies and sell them because we get attached to certain ones. We hadn't planned on having so many dogs, but Lucy, Oxie, and Nicki are pups that came from different litters. They were so cute we wanted them to stay with us. Some dogs you can't part with although they would bring in money. A dog's companionship and love are sometimes worth more than the money. Selling one of those dogs would be like selling a family member.

SEAN: I'M THE MIDDLE KID in the family. Sometimes it feels like I get the short end of the stick. Other times I like where I am in the family.

Dusty is the youngest, so he gets lots of attention. D.C. is the oldest. He gets all A's in school. My grades aren't as good as his, but I do more work around the farm than D.C. does, and I enjoy doing it. I love having lots of animals.

I enjoy helping to plant the vegetables and herbs in the spring. We grow everything organically, and my mom makes everything from scratch. We sell the herbs to a Thai restaurant, Star of Siam. Lots of people we've never met eat the herbs when they order food at the restaurant. It makes me feel good that our farm touches so many people.

I also love to help my mom cook. Just about every evening, I help her make dinner. If she wants somebody to help cut up

Left to right: DANIEL (DAD), ONE OF THE COLLIES, D.C., LOIS (MOM), DUSTY, SEAN

onions or anything else, she knows that I'm available. I even help her with the canning each year.

One good thing about being in the middle is that I have two brothers to play with—one younger and one older. When D.C. and I play games like basketball with Dusty, we give him extra points. That makes me feel grown-up.

I'm too young to do certain things with D.C., like go to dances. But I'm old enough to sell cards at the flea market with him. So I guess my place in the family is pretty good. Instead of just being the middle one, I'm the second oldest one, too. I have one brother I can look up to and another brother that looks up to me. That's okay.

DUSTY: MY MOM CALLS ME her outdoorsman. I guess I am. I spend more time with the animals than anyone else. We don't just have dogs. We have sheep, chickens, and geese. The geese honk when any strangers come around. They're better watchdogs than all of our dogs put together. Collies aren't an aggressive breed of dog, and ours aren't barkers. We didn't get the collies for protection anyway. We just want to play with them and love them. One thing I love best is "dancing" with Lisa. She'll stand on her hind legs and put her paws on my shoulders and we'll cuddle and pretend to dance. She's a very smart dog. You tell her not to step on the flowers in our garden and she won't!

Being the youngest means I'm not old enough to do the things that Sean and D.C. do. I don't go to dances or sleepovers. But I don't mind at all. And I don't get lonely when my brothers go places. I like staying at home with my parents and the animals.

No matter what, I always have animals to play with. One of our sheep just had lambs, so I've been playing with them a lot lately. The black one is my favorite. I call him Blackie.

I also help in the businesses. I love raising the dogs. I also go to flea markets and sell items. I don't sell cards, though. I sell trolls. I don't make as much money as D.C. or Sean. But that's okay with me. I'm expanding to pogs. That's where the market seems to be going, so maybe one day I'll make as much as my brothers.

Meghan

AGE 11

Some families have parents with different religious beliefs.

MEGHAN: MY NAME IS Meghan O'Connor. So when people first meet me, they think I'm Irish Catholic. I'm not! My mom is Jewish and my dad is Lutheran. My Dad's great-great-grandfather was Irish, so I just have a teeny-tiny bit of Irish blood.

My mother observes her religion more than my dad does. So she's told me more about being Jewish. That's the religion I practice. I go to Hebrew School twice a week and to Sabbath School on Saturday mornings. Sabbath School is like Sunday School except that it happens on Saturday, the Jewish day of rest. The Jewish Sabbath begins at sundown on Friday and lasts until sundown on Saturday.

My mom and I go to Friday evening services often. My dad always goes, too. Even though he's never converted to Judaism, he's a member of our congregation and very active in it. The synagogue my family belongs to has many families where one parent is Jewish and one is Christian. Lots of my parents' friends are in mixed marriages. When I was little, I used to think all families had one Christian and one Jewish parent.

Although I don't practice being Lutheran, I do participate in certain Christian holidays—the ones my dad celebrates. My dad doesn't go to church on Sundays, but sometimes we go to church on Christmas and Easter. My mom and I don't kneel or participate in the service. We listen to the minister and the music.

Meghan

At Christmastime, my family celebrates both Christmas and Hanukkah, the Jewish festival of lights. Although both holidays fall near each other, Hanukkah is not the Jewish Christmas. It's actually a minor Jewish holiday during which families light candles and give gifts. It became a big celebration in the United States because it's so near Christmas. But my family celebrates Hanukkah like most American Jews, with lots of festivities and gifts. And every year, my parents give a huge Hanukkah-Christmas party for both their families at our house.

Since we celebrate both holidays, we put up a Christmas tree around Thanksgiving and light our menorah during Hanukkah. A menorah is a candelabra with nine spaces in it. Hanukkah lasts eight nights. Each evening, another candle is added, and I get presents from my parents.

On Christmas, I get lots of presents from my dad and his relatives. This annoys my mom, because it seems like everybody tries to outdo everyone—and that's not what Christmas or Hanukkah is about.

In the spring, we celebrate Passover. Passover lasts a week. On the first two nights, Jewish people have a dinner called a Seder. We have a limited number of people at our Seder because our dining room table only seats twelve. A Seder is a sit-down dinner, not a buffet like we have for our

Clockwise from top: CHUCK (DAD), ELYSE (MOM), COURTNEY THE COLLIE, MEGHAN

Hanukkah-Christmas celebration. If my father's mother is in town, she attends.

When I grow up, I'll decide which religion I want to practice. For now it's fun to be exposed to many different people and experiences, although I still feel like I'd rather be Jewish.

Nathan, Nicholas, and Adam

AGES 12, 11, AND 9

Some families have people with disabilities.

NATHAN: I'M THE OLDEST in my family. Sometimes I like it, and sometimes it isn't much fun. Like I might want to act goofy, and I'll have to watch myself because I need to set an example for my two younger brothers and my sister, Ahnalieza, who's two. (We call her Ahna.) It's very tempting to act goofy at times, especially with Nic. He's a year younger than me. When my mom takes us to a store to buy clothes, the two of us get really silly. We like to play hide-and-seek between the clothing racks.

Since I'm the oldest, I have to compromise a lot. When Nic needs to use our room to do his homework, I have to let him use our desk. Sometimes Nic and I argue over stuff like what to watch on TV. That's something we try not to argue over very much. If we really get serious about the argument, Mom or Dad makes us turn off the TV. Then neither of us watches anything. So TV spats aren't worth it.

Adam is my youngest brother. He's nine and has Down syndrome.* My Mom says he's a blessing—and she's right. Because of Adam, it's easy to accept all kinds of people.

Adam can't do everything Nic and I do. He can't play sports

Clockwise from top: GREG (DAD), NATHAN, ADAM (SEATED AT COMPUTER), NICHOLAS

as well as Nic and I. He doesn't have the skills and may never have them. So Nic and I change the rules when we play with Adam to make things easier for him. When we play basketball, we let Adam take double dribbles and we lower the net for him. We don't play as well as we would otherwise. Sometimes we even pretend to fall down.

Adam has to be careful about riding his bike. He can't ride it in the street. I go with him sometimes so he can use his bicycle. I'm very careful to make sure Adam rides on the road near our house. Lots of times I feel like I need to protect Adam because he's younger and has a disability.

Sometimes Adam can be a pest. He'll want to play with me when I'm not in the mood. He'll really bug me about it, too. Adam has a stubborn streak and doesn't give up easily. But I know that any other nine-year-old brother would be like Adam is, in that way.

---

* Down syndrome is a chromosome disorder that usually causes a delay in physical, intellectual, and language development. It usually results in mental retardation.

NICHOLAS: Since I'm younger and don't have as much homework as Nate has, I have more time to play with Adam and Ahna. So I like being second oldest. I like to play with Adam and Ahna's toys, especially Adam's little men and their garage. I like Ahna's Lite Brite, too. It's fun when Ahna, Adam, and I all play with it together.

Adam can do lots of things even though he has Down syndrome. Sometimes I help Adam with his reading. That makes me feel good about both of us. I'm helping him to learn. Adam's in a special class at our school. When he sees Nate or me on the playground, he's always happy to see us and know we're there. So we wave to him and he waves back.

Our dog, Casey, likes Adam the best. We got Casey after Adam was born. Casey follows Adam everywhere. My mom says, "Casey senses that Adam needs special attention." That sure seems to be true. We consider Casey a pet and an important family member.

Clockwise from top left: GREG (DAD), NATHAN, NICHOLAS, CASEY THE DOG, MARIANNE (MOM) HOLDING AHNA, ADAM

Sometimes little kids make fun of Adam because he doesn't speak clearly. Adam is pretty good at taking care of himself, though. He'll just say "Go away!" when anybody upsets him. And kids usually do go away when he tells them to. I think

Adam has found a good way of handling the situation. But Adam also says "Go away!" to me and Nate if he gets mad at us. Adam gets mad at us when he doesn't want to share in chores, like helping us clean out the garage.

My sister Ahna is very cute. All of us were excited when she was born. We hadn't had a little sister before. Ahna does funny things, like bang on the piano.

Not long ago, Ahna needed heart surgery. I was scared for her and happy, too. I knew the surgery would make her well, but it was kind of scary that she'd be going into the hospital for a serious operation. Adam, Nate, and I all stayed at my grandparents' house. They live over an hour away from us, and most of my aunts, uncles, and cousins live near them. My mother has fifteen brothers and sisters. I have forty-three cousins. So when we visit my grandparents, we also see lots of other relatives.

We got to take time off from school while Ahna was in the hospital. I liked that. I was glad to see Ahna when she got out. Nate, Adam, and my parents gave her a stuffed dog that looks just like Casey for a homecoming present. She loved that—and so did Adam.

ADAM: MY FAMILY DOES lots of things together. I like it best when we go camping together. I love helping to make the campfire. It's fun to build the campfire with my dad and brothers.

I also love to play Candyland with Nate and Nic. I play a lot with Ahna, too. We share a bunk bed. I'm on top. Ahna and I play with a wooden train and a hospital with little plastic people.

When I was little, my family bought Casey, our dog. He was my dog at first. He followed me around and made sure I didn't leave the yard. I don't do that anymore, so now Casey is everybody's dog. Even though he hangs around me the most, he loves everyone and is an important family member.

Susan and Maria

AGES 14 AND 12

Some families have relatives who live in other countries.

SUSAN: IT'S ALL GIRLS at my house. My sister and I live with my mom. My parents are divorced. We call my dad a lot and see him on weekends. So even though my folks are divorced, we see our dad often and are very close to him.

My mom works, and when she's at work I'm in charge. Sometimes that's hard because Maria doesn't always listen to me when I tell her to do things, like her homework. I guess it's a natural reaction, though, since I'm only two years older than her. I probably wouldn't listen well if I were in the same situation. Still, when Maria does that, it bugs me.

Sometimes Maria and I cook dinner together. I know how to make barbecued chicken and pork. I'd like to learn how to make some authentic Chinese dishes and know more about my culture. My sister and I were both born here and are very American.

We're Buddhists, but we still celebrate holidays like Christmas and Easter, and we celebrate both the Christian and Chinese New Years. During Chinese New Year we dress in new clothes and visit all my mom's relatives. Then we usually all go to Chinatown. That's an

Left to right: SUSAN, ANGEL (MOM), MARIA

area in our town where lots of Chinese people live. There are lots of Chinese restaurants and shops in Chinatown, too. The annual Chinese New Year parade occurs there and we watch it together.

My dad's relatives live in Hong Kong. He may take us to Hong Kong in the near future to visit his relatives. I think it will be exciting to meet people who live thousands of miles away that I haven't seen before.

I'm especially looking forward to meeting my father's brother, Uncle Anthony, who lives in Hong Kong. I've written to him and he's written to us for years. He's sent us gifts from Hong Kong, like a puzzle of the city. We've seen each other's pictures, too, and talked on the phone. But even if I'd never seen a picture of Uncle Anthony, I think I'd know who he was when I stepped off the plane. I know him so well from our letters it's like we've already met.

MARIA: MY MOM AND SISTER and I have special things that just the three of us do together. When we're at home, my mom will turn on the radio and listen to Chinese music. She'll dance and we'll copy her. It's kind of neat being able to do something together that's part of our culture. It makes the three of us feel unique and closer together.

Sometimes I argue with Susan. She gets mad at me for borrowing her clothes. We also have conflicts about using the phone. If we're mad at each other after dinner, we'll do the dishes and continue the argument by throwing water at each other. But no matter how angry we are, we'll usually make up by the time we go to bed. But sometimes we've had some big spats that lasted longer than that.

Sometimes Susan and I just argue to argue—over nothing big. Let's say that I'm sitting quietly watching TV. Susan will complain that I'm boring and tease me, or I'll do the same thing to her. It's just how we interact. I know that lots of brothers and sisters near the same age do the same thing. And although Susan and I argue, I'd rather have a sister near my age than be an only child. That seems super boring!

Sometimes my mom, Susan, and I go to the mall together and shop. We'll buy clothes and stop at the Old Country Buffet before we go home. Sometimes the three of us visit Chinatown and eat at one of the restaurants. I love ordering barbecued ribs, Peking duck, and Chinese chicken. I wonder what kind of Chinese food they serve in Hong Kong, and someday soon I'll know, because of the trip my dad has planned for us.

I'm really looking forward to the trip to Hong Kong with my dad. We'll meet all his relatives and see China. It's amazing that you can have people related to you living thousands of miles away whom you've never met before—but still you're connected.

Last year my Aunt Nancy came to visit from Hong Kong. We went to the airport with my dad to meet her. Of course, we were pretty sure who she was when we saw her. She was the only Chinese person waiting at the airport gate. Then we introduced ourselves and hugged—just like we'd known each other forever. That felt pretty terrific.

Eric and Erica

AGES 12 AND 9

Some families have parents who are divorced, yet the parents still have a good relationship.

ERIC: ALTHOUGH MY PARENTS are divorced, I'm lucky about my family situation. I live with my mom and my sister, Erica. Of course, I wish my parents weren't divorced. But we see our dad at least every other weekend and during the week. He's welcome to drop by whenever he wants. My mom and dad respect each other and get along well. They just can't live together. My mom says, "Sometimes that happens."

This doesn't mean that my folks will get back together. I know they won't. But I think I'm very fortunate that my folks are divorced and still get along. Some kids' parents get divorced and they don't see the other parent much—or their parents can barely say a kind word to each other or about each other.

My grandfather lives in our house, too. He and his girlfriend, Eleanor, have an apartment downstairs. Mom, my grandfather, Erica, Eleanor, and I eat dinner together every night. My mom makes dinner or we'll order in. That's one of my favorite times of day. Not just because we're eating, but because we all have a chance to be together and talk. We discuss school, my mom's work, the news, and even what the dogs did that was funny or cute. Between the five of us, there could be lots of different conversations starting and stopping. If the weather is nice, we go out after dinner and sit on the porch together. Then we continue our conversations.

The five of us love to play cards—poker and Crazy Eights. Lots of evenings during the summer, we'll play until it's time for bed. When school's on, my grandfather helps me with my math homework. My mom's good in math, too. She works at a bank, but I like my grandfather to help me. It gives us a chance for the two of us to be alone together. I think my grandfather is a very special person. Sometimes he'll tell me about the things he did as a kid—the mischief and the good stuff.

My mom, Erica, and I love movies. Just about every weekend, the three of us see one. Sometimes we'll see a first-run movie. Sometimes we'll see a movie at the neighborhood theater for a dollar fifty, or we'll rent a movie.

Left to right: ERIC, ERICA, KARLA (MOM)

My dad likes movies, too. So when we visit him, we often go to the movies. He loves movies so much that he owns almost two hundred videos.

One of the things that seems to happen a lot at my house is that I argue with Erica. We'll bicker about really stupid stuff, like who gets to use the remote control for the TV set. And I have to admit, I sometimes enjoy arguing with Erica. Sometimes we won't even be mad at each other, but we'll argue to argue and even laugh about it. It can be kind of entertaining.

Yesterday Erica went to visit a friend. It was quiet at home for a while. That was okay for a few hours. But after a while it was too quiet, and I wished that Erica was around to play with or have a friendly argument with.

ERICA: BESIDES THE PEOPLE in my house, there are the dogs, too—Heather and Gizmo. Gizmo is my grandfather's dog. He's small. Heather's our dog. Sometimes she gets me into trouble with my grandfather. She'll follow me into his apartment and eat Gizmo's food. Then Grandpa will get mad and I'll start to cry. But Eleanor will smooth things over. Then I don't feel so bad.

Usually my grandfather and Eleanor are very nice to us. They'll play cards with us and teach us card tricks. If I have a bad day at school, I'll go home and tell my grandfather. He'll talk it over with me and joke about it. Then I'll get over feeling bad. Grandpa's retired, so he's home all the time and there for Eric and me. When my mom's not home, I know there are adults around, so Eric and I never feel alone or scared.

Even though our dad doesn't live with us, we see him regularly. He drops by for surprise visits. That makes me feel good. My dad and mom are friends even though they're divorced. I've told my mom that I wish that they'd get back together, like some of my friends' parents have. But she says, "I just can't do that." Still, I'm lucky that both my parents get along and we see Dad a lot.

My mom does a lot of things with us. Last year, my mom and I, Eric, and a cousin of mine all went to Disney World together. That was fun. In the summer, Mom sets up our pool in the yard and we all go swimming.

My family has a special routine we do about once a month on a Sunday. My mom, my grandfather, Eric, Eleanor, and I go to Dappers for dinner. It's sort of a fancy restaurant, so we don't go there very often. It makes me feel good that we're all together doing something that special.

On holidays, we'll have a big feast. My mom makes turkey, corn, ham, stuffing, and lots of other food. My dad might drop by, or we'll go over to his place. My parents don't have a strict arrangement, like "you saw the kids last weekend, so you can't see them this holiday or weekend." They're relaxed about stuff like that. So I guess I'm lucky that they get along and Eric and I see our dad a lot. Since my grandfather, Eleanor, and the two dogs live here, there's always something interesting going on. Eric and I always have people to be with and fun things to do.

Jonathan, Natalie, and Christopher

AGES 10, 12, AND 12

Some families have parents who are the same gender.

JONATHAN: I FEEL LIKE I have two moms—and I might have a third one soon.

Most of the year, my brother, sister, and I live with my mom, who is a lesbian, and Barb, her partner. In the summer, Chris, Natalie, and I spend six weeks with my dad. Now he's dating a lady named Katie, and he's probably going to marry her soon. So that's why I feel like I might almost have three moms.

I'm not supposed to talk about Barb with my dad or Katie with my mom. My dad says, "Whatever happens at someone else's house is their private business." Nobody I know seems to care that my mom is a lesbian. They've never said anything about her or Barb.

My mom says, "Living in our neighborhood makes our family seem more acceptable. People are more open to different lifestyles in our kind of neighborhood." We live in Hyde Park near the University of Chicago. So we see people from many different cultures and lifestyles.

Clockwise from left: PEGGY (MOM), JONATHAN, CHRISTOPHER, BARBARA (PEGGY'S PARTNER), NATALIE

My older brother Christopher and my sister Natalie are twins. When I was younger, I wished that I could be a twin, too. But now I'm glad to be who I am. Actually, I feel like I'm the luckiest kid in my family.

Chris and Natalie both have asthma—and Chris has a learning disability. He has a hard time writing things down on paper, so he's in a special class at school.

Sometimes kids make fun of Chris. They say, "You're a nerd." That's because Chris wears thick glasses and he's skinny. That makes me feel bad because Chris can't help how he looks.

So I guess I'm pretty lucky in general. I don't have asthma, wear glasses, or go to a special class. I kind of have two moms, maybe a third one soon—and a dad. I also like being the youngest one in my family.

NATALIE: I LIKE LIVING with my mom and Barb. Barb, my mom's partner, is an important part of our family. She's kind of like a stepmom. Barb lets us do things that my mom won't let us do very often.

Barb lets us stay up later than my mom does—and lets us watch more television. When I go shopping with Barb, she'll buy things like marshmallow fluff and cookies. Those are things my mom doesn't like me to have very often. I guess Barb is a little easier with all of us because she doesn't have kids of her own.

One of my two best friends, Jill, knows that Mom and Barb are lesbians. Sometimes Jill asks questions. When my mom wears a T-shirt that says something about being gay or a lesbian, Jill asks questions like, "Why is your mom wearing that shirt?" I'll just say, "It's because she likes it." I don't go on about Mom and Barb being lesbians.

My other best friend, Tracy, knows. Her mom is a lesbian, too. So Tracy kind of likes it because that means there's someone like her. I like that, too.

Barb has lived with my mom and my brothers and me for the last three years. Our family wouldn't seem whole without Barb. Like once we planned a trip to visit my great-grandfather. He doesn't know that my mom is a lesbian, so Barb felt funny about coming along. She didn't go on the trip. It wasn't as much fun as it could have been because Barb wasn't there.

Even though my family is different, they are normal to me—and I love doing things with them. And I don't know what we'd do without Barb living with us. She's very important to all of us.

CHRISTOPHER: I'M A TWIN, but I'm not an identical twin. So I think of Natalie more as a plain sister, not my twin.

I'm eighteen minutes older, but Natalie tries to always be the boss. That's how she's always been. Sometimes I think that she's the bossiest person in my entire family—or the bossiest person I ever met. Also, she can sure hold a grudge. If she gets mad, it's for a few days. Jonathan just gets mad for a few minutes, so I'd rather play with him.

Sometimes, if Natalie and I are in a really big fight, Barb or my mom force us to make up. Mom knows how to get Natalie and me talking and playing again. Barb is pretty good at it, too. Natalie and I argue a lot, so I guess Barb got used to us.

Living with Barb and Mom is better than when my mom and dad lived together. They argued a lot. I like having Barb here better than being with Mom by herself. I think it's good to have two adults in a house. I always know that somebody will make dinner and help me with my homework, even if one person is busy or not home yet.

To me, it doesn't matter who lives with me, as long as they treat me, Jonathan, Natalie, and Mom okay.

Lindsey and Heather

Ages 10 and 11

Some families have people of different races.

LINDSEY: Since my mother is Caucasian and my dad is African-American, I'm biracial. I'm half African-American and half Caucasian. That's exactly how I feel. I'm not more one race than another.

Once when we took a standardized test at school, I needed to fill in a space that asked which race I was. There were spaces for African-American, Caucasian, Asian, and Hispanic. My teacher made me fill in the space for African-American. I didn't think that space was really correct, and the incident made me upset. I'm just as much Caucasian as I am African-American, so I should have filled in the *two* spaces. Or the test company should have printed the test with a space for biracial.

The town where I live is mostly Caucasian, but my being biracial isn't a big deal to the kids I know. They just accept me for who I am. Still, my mom always talks about moving to another suburb where there are people from many different racial backgrounds. She'd like me and my sister to know people from other cultures, especially other African-Americans.

Left to right: LINDSEY, DEWITT (DAD), DEBBIE (MOM), HEATHER

Even without being biracial, my family is unusual. My sister and I are probably the only kids I know who have somebody from their family around them almost all the time. My mom works at my school. We live in a two-family house. My mom, dad, sister, and I live on the second floor. My mom's sister, Aunt Jeanne, my Uncle Dick, and two older cousins live on the first floor.

My sister and I haven't ever had a baby-sitter who wasn't a family member, because we've always had so many family members living in the same house. My Aunt Jeanne and Uncle Dick are fun to be with. They really relate to kids. I can tell my cousin Chrissy, who is sixteen, lots of things. Chrissy is old enough to seem grown-up but still young enough so that I can trust her like I would another kid. I can talk to her about things that I wouldn't tell a *real* grown-up.

I usually like living near lots of family members, but I'm not always so thrilled about having my mom work at my school.

She's an aide for a boy who's autistic. She's been at my school for a long time and knows all the teachers.

Sometimes my mom drops into my classroom to say hello. That's so embarrassing! Other times it's not so bad having my mom at school. A few times I forgot my lunch money, and once I got sick at school—so my mom was there to fix everything. Then having my mom around was absolutely awesome!

HEATHER: SINCE I'M DARK-COMPLECTED and thin, kids who don't know me are kind of surprised to meet my mom. She's a redhead, short, and a different body type than my sister and my dad. My sister, my dad, and I are all tall and thin. Kids don't ask any questions about my mom, but they wonder about her. I'd be curious if I met somebody who had a mom that looked so different.

I like being both Caucasian and African-American. I knew a lot about Dr. Martin Luther King, Jr., before most other kids at school did. My folks had already discussed what an important person he was.

My mom teaches Sunday School at our church. My church has members from lots of different backgrounds. Every winter, my mom holds a class about Kwanzaa, an African-American holiday that happens from December 26th through January 2nd. It makes me feel so proud that *my* mother teaches the class. Next spring, she is going to teach a class on Juneteenth, a holiday that celebrates freedom from slavery.

Once, though, a boy made fun of my sister because she's half African-American. He called her a bad word. When I told my mom, she said, "Whatever he called her didn't have much to do with her being part African-American. He must have felt bad about himself. People with good self-esteem don't make fun of other people."

My biggest problems don't have to do with being biracial. They usually have to do with my sister, Lindsey. She's younger, but she has a very strong personality. When I bring friends over, she almost always has to join us—and she's good at horning in. Sometimes she ends up playing with my friends more than I do. That makes me so mad!

I like being part of two different cultures. I'm used to it. I don't know what it would be like to be part of only one culture, so I can't really compare it.

Left to right: HEATHER AND LINDSEY

And although Lindsey sometimes steals my friends, I'm glad I have a sister near my age. I usually have someone to play with and talk to, so I'm hardly ever lonely.

Jake and Tom

AGES 11 AND 12

Some families live in group homes.

JAKE: My brother and I live in a great big house with about forty other kids. It's a group home. The house is divided into apartments with three bedrooms apiece. I share one of these rooms with Tom, my big brother, and another kid my age named Bob. Nine kids live in the apartment, and we've become very close—almost like brothers. The guys in the apartment all eat at the same table in the home's dining room and do chores together, like keep our apartment clean. A house parent is in charge of us.

When I first came to the home, I missed Tom. He was living someplace else. I was sure glad a year later when he came to live here, too. But even without Tom living here, I thought the home was pretty okay.

The people at the home gave me a bike when I first arrived. I can ride it in the parking lot or around the block. The guys here

Jake and Tom are not the real names of the boys who tell their stories here. Because they live in a group home, their names have been changed to protect their privacy, and they were not allowed to be photographed.

play scatterball, too. That's a game where somebody tosses a ball, then everyone rushes to catch it and stands very still. We play Army, Navy, and Marines, too. We pretend we've joined the service and act like soldiers.

There are rules at the home, like we can't fight with the other kids or do lots of whining. If you break the rules, you'll get points against you. When that happens, you have to go to bed early or do extra chores like clean up somebody else's room. It's best to follow the rules here, so I try hard to stay out of trouble.

TOM: I LIKE IT HERE a lot at the home. Living here has given me a chance to have lots of experiences I wouldn't otherwise have. During the summer, I go to sleepover camp in another state. I canoe and fish at camp. I know I wouldn't have the chance to do that in many other situations—and neither would lots of other kids.

The kids at the home visit places like Great America. We go to baseball games and basketball games, too. Once a year, a professional football player comes to visit all the kids who live here. I'm sure that no matter where else I lived, no famous ballplayer is going to end up on my doorstep.

It's wise to follow the rules at the home, because then you'll get lots of treats like candy, popcorn, and a bigger allowance. If you break the rules, then your allowance will get docked, and I don't like that. So I try to follow the rules.

I've made lots of friends here, but Jake and I won't be here forever. We could go to a private foster home with a family or get adopted. Or we could be transferred to a facility for older children. For now, I hope we just stay here. My brother and I are used to it, and we like the stuff that goes on here.

When a kid leaves the home, we have a closing party where everyone says good-bye. It's sad for everyone. Some kids cry. You can really get close to kids here. Even though they aren't relatives, they become like family. You live with them every day, so you become close.

Whenever there is a closing party, I think about what it might be like when I leave the home. I'm sure other kids do, too. I've been told that when Jake or I leave, we'll be going together. We won't get split up. That's good. We're blood family and should be together no matter where we go.

Laura and Amanda

AGES 14 AND 9

Some families have people who come from many different places.

LAURA: MY FAMILY IS quite amazing. I have a brother and two sisters who are adopted, and each of them came from someplace else. Yet we're all a family. That seems pretty super when I stop to think about it.

Amanda is from Evanston, Illinois, my hometown. Joey is from Romania, and Sarah, my youngest sister, is from Ohio. Soon we'll have a new sister. She's coming from China. It's fun having a brother and sisters and being the oldest, except when I have to baby-sit.

Amanda really looks up to me and wants to be like me. Sometimes I put lipstick on her or polish her nails. We look very similar, so sometimes people don't believe she's adopted.

My friends think Amanda is cute—and she is. She's also good at not hanging around or tagging along when I want to be alone with my friends.

Sarah, my youngest sister, is two. She's biracial. Like Amanda, she came to us when she was an infant, just like a biological brother or sister would. So both Amanda and Sarah's arrival was pretty much like the arrival of anybody else's brother or sister. The day they came home was the first time I saw either of them.

JOEY AND HIS DAD, JOSEPH

Joey's arrival was very different. He came to us from Romania when he was two years old, and we had an actual preview of him. We watched a video of Joey before my parents brought him home.

My parents had seen a TV program that told about the thousands of children in Romania that were orphaned. Then they visited Romania to adopt a child. My mom had to stay in Romania for about two months before she could bring Joey home. So she had a video of Joey made and sent it to us while she was still in Romania.

Joey had been neglected in Romania. He'd lived in an overcrowded orphanage with little attention. When he came to us, he couldn't walk or talk. Although he's able to walk now, nobody knows for sure if he'll ever be able to talk.

My friends try to talk to Joey, hug him, and give him attention. Of course, my sisters do that too, especially Sarah. Sarah is very outgoing. She'll just pull Joey over and expect him to play with her. She won't be satisfied until Joey is interacting with her somehow. She's the most outgoing of my sisters, and she won't take no for an answer.

AMANDA: It's awesome that the kids in my family are from so many places. I think that Joey is the most amazing one. I almost couldn't believe our family would have a brother from that far away until I saw the video. Soon we'll have a sister from China. The agency will send the picture. I can't wait to see it.

I like having brothers and sisters who are older, younger, and from so many places. I always have somebody to play with. I can be a big or little sister, depending on who I'm with.

I can go to the movies with Laura and ride bikes with her. Sometimes I wear her outgrown clothes. When she's wearing things I like, I hope I'll wear them someday. But usually I'm happier to have new clothes.

Clockwise from top: JOSEPH (DAD), AMANDA, JOEY, CAROL (MOM), SARAH, LAURA

I enjoy playing dress-up with Sarah and playing with her toys. She's very outgoing and loves to play.

I like to take Joey to the park. I'll push him on the swings. Sometimes people think he's weird because he can't talk. But that doesn't mean he can't play or communicate. He can. Joey lets you know what he wants by pointing or taking your hand to lead you to what he wants or needs. He has his own way of telling people things.

One thing neat about our family is that not everyone has just a birthday celebration. My adopted siblings and I have a coming home day, too. My birthday is in April, but I didn't come home until mid-June. I was premature and had to stay in the hospital. So I have a regular birthday party and a coming home day, too. On our coming home day, Mom makes our favorite food or takes us to a museum.

I like being in a family with people from so many places. I'm very lucky to be adopted into my family. If I'd been born into it, that would be lucky, too.

Zinta and Erika

AGES 10 AND 8

Some families have parents who aren't married to each other.

ZINTA: I LIVE WITH my mom, my sister Erika, and two cats, Dusty and Bernice. Daddy lives with us, too. He's not our real dad. He's our mom's boyfriend. Daddy lives with us most of the time, but not always. He's a poet, so he needs a quiet space of his own. He has his own apartment a few blocks away. That's where he does his writing.

We see our real dad, who we call Papa, about twice a year. He lives far away in Arizona. Erika and I take the plane by ourselves to visit him. It makes us feel very grown-up.

Daddy is different from our real father. Our real father likes to do things outside a lot, like play on the swings and go to the park. Daddy is more of an indoor person. He plays his guitar for us. Every night, we have a jam session. Daddy plays his guitar. Erika, my mom, and I dance to the tunes. My favorite song is "Go Johnny Go."

My sister and I don't watch TV very often. We do things, listen to the guitar, and read at night after we do our homework. Sometimes it's hard to talk to other kids because they're so interested in television. Even though I don't watch a lot of TV, I do things other kids never do. My sister and I have our own art room. We have crayons, stickers, beads, markers, paint, fabric, and all kinds of paper. We can make a huge mess in that room as long as we clean it up on Saturday. I'm sure other kids don't have a room that they can mess up. Erika and I like to get up early and play in there most days before we leave for school.

Erika and I have a special game called Secret Garden. We play Secret Garden almost every day. We arrange our miniature plastic horses, sea shells, rocks, and dried flowers in special ways. Then we act out parts from a story that we make up.

Sometimes all four of us go to Barnes and Noble, a bookstore that has a café in it. Either Mom or Daddy buys us a book. Then we have a treat at the café. That's fun.

This summer, my mother, my sister, and I are going on an adventure. My mom is going to be the cook at a Girl Scout camp in Maryland. We're going with her. My aunt is the director of the camp. Dusty and Bernice will stay home with Daddy. I'll miss them, but I know Daddy will take very good care of them.

Left to right: KAREN (MOM), TERRY ("DADDY"), ERIKA, ZINTA

ERIKA: My family isn't exactly like other families. Even our cats are individuals. They've picked out which family members they want to hang out with.

Dusty is very friendly to Daddy and my mom. He's the adults' cat. Bernice likes Zinta and me. Bernice lets us dress her up in doll clothes and carry her around. She kind of ignores Daddy and Mom. So she's the kids' cat. Zinta and I like her the best.

We only have one tiny TV set. So we do other things like playing in our art room. My real father works in television. But even when we lived with him, we didn't watch TV a lot. He liked to build things with me and my sister. Once he made a huge building out of our blocks that went up to the ceiling.

Once a month, Daddy, my sister, Mom, and I all go downtown to the Luna Café. My Mom and Daddy go to poetry club meetings there. We have a friend our age that we see when we go to the club. Her name is Dorothy, and her parents own the café. While our parents are at the meeting, we sit by the window and look outside together. It's fun to watch people walk by.

When we're with Dorothy, we usually make food out of clay. Zinta and I like to make ice cream cones and hamburgers. We don't eat hamburgers very often. My mother is pretty much a vegetarian, so we rarely have meat at our house. This doesn't mean that Zinta and I never eat it. We buy lunch at school and it often has meat in it. Sometimes we even go to McDonald's and Mom buys us hamburgers. She says that just because she has her own ideas about things, that doesn't mean we have to think the same way. If we couldn't have a hamburger at McDonald's, it wouldn't really be going to McDonald's. My mom is good about letting us have our own ideas, even though we're kids. She knows we think about things, too.

I like the adventures we have with Daddy and Mom. I'm glad Daddy is part of our family, too. And I'm glad my mom lets us have our own ideas about things.

Mark and Ryan

AGES 16 AND 19

Some families have
crises they need to handle.

MARK: MY FAMILY IS what you call "take charge" and up front about things. They know the best way to handle a crisis is to turn to the Lord for help. When I turned thirteen, I was diagnosed with leukemia, which is a cancer of the blood. The minute I was diagnosed, my mom called my dad at work and my brother at school—right from the doctor's office. She called our relatives and friends, too. She felt by reacting this way, people could begin praying for us, so we would have the strength and support we needed while the four of us dealt with my illness.

I began chemotherapy immediately after I was diagnosed. When anyone receives chemotherapy, strong chemicals are given to them to kill their cancer cells. The chemicals are actually poisons, and I didn't react well to them at all. The chemotherapy almost caused kidney failure. So I was in intensive care for a few days. Since then, I've had a couple more hospital stays and many trips to the clinic for my treatments.

My mom or dad were always at the hospital. They'd take different shifts so I wouldn't have to be by myself in the hospital and face being sick alone. When I got home from the hospital, my brother Ryan always watched out for me. He'd bring me my dinner and get my work from school. He'd always ask me how I was. Ryan was a tremendous support.

Besides being my father, my dad was my basketball coach. So the entire team rallied around our family. The guys on the team knew that the chemotherapy would make me lose my hair. They didn't want me to feel different when I got back, so they shaved their heads, too. That made me feel like everyone was behind me—and that my teammates were like family.

Although I had a serious illness, many good things happened to my family because of it. The head-shaving incident made lots of newspapers. The articles resulted in lots of letters. Our family was interviewed on the "Home Show," and the show sent us to a Bulls game, where I was a ball boy. An organization called "Make a Wish" sent the four of us to Hawaii. In Hawaii, Ryan and I joked about how my illness made the trip possible.

MARK WITH PHOTOGRAPHS FROM HIS CHEMOTHERAPY DAYS

Clockwise from top left: MARK, TIM (DAD), RYAN, MARCIA (MOM)

My illness has made me grateful for every day I have, and for being part of such a close and God-fearing family. It brought us all closer together, and it made me realize that bad things can sometimes happen to any family. But by trusting in the Lord for healing and knowing He's in control, the bad things will turn into positive things. It depends on how everyone deals with them.

RYAN: WHEN MARK WAS first diagnosed with leukemia, I was shocked. My mom called me at school. She didn't wait until I got home to tell me in person. But that's how both my parents are. If there's something important going on, they don't hide it. They want us to know about it right away.

It was scary knowing that Mark had leukemia. And I couldn't see him every day, since he was in the hospital. The hospital was far from our house, so I could only visit him when rides and schedule conflicts were worked out. We talked on the phone, but sometimes Mark wasn't even well enough to hold a conversation. I missed having Mark around to talk to and argue with. Since my parents went to the hospital a lot, sometimes I felt isolated and disrupted. It kind of put a crimp in my sports and school activities.

Mark's leukemia made me appreciate him more when he returned home. I realized how fortunate I was to have a brother near my age. The leukemia also made me see how fast things can change, and it made me realize how comforting it is to live in a normal family with ordinary things happening.

This fall I went to college. Of course, I missed Mark and the rest of the family, and I thought about Mark a lot. Every time I'd get a call late in the evening and hear one of my parents' voices over the phone, I'd feel scared. You'd never know what the call was about, and at first I would think the worst. I'd think something had happened to Mark. But he's been fine and in a solid remission.

The calls didn't have anything to do with Mark's illness. The calls were from my folks, but they were just about typical stuff— neighborhood happenings, family gossip, or what might have happened at church. It was my parents' way of saying, "You're not here, but we'll keep you posted on the goings-on." Those are good calls, and I love getting them.

Elizabeth, Jeff, Sam, Kelly, and Mike

AGES 15, 14, 12, 11, AND 10

Some families have lots of kids.

ELIZABETH: I'M PART OF a big family—eleven kids in all. It's fun. I'm never lonely, and I always have somebody around to talk to and be with. I don't have anything else to compare it to, but my dad does. He was an only child and didn't like it, so he wanted a big family.

Four of us are our parents' biological children and seven of us are adopted. Six of us are from Korea. But we were all very young when we were adopted, so none of us remembers living anywhere else. My mom has offered to take those of us born in Korea for a visit, but the only one interested so far is Kelly. To me, the United States is home, and I don't feel a connection with Korea. I'd rather go to Europe if I were going on a big trip.

I like having brothers and sisters both older and younger—and near my age. My sister Molly is eighteen. We share clothes and go

Only five of the eleven kids in Elizabeth's family were interviewed for this book because the family is so large. The other family members (besides Mom and Dad) are Drew, 28; Katie, 26; Bill, 24; Matt, 23; Molly, 18; and Anna, 6.

shopping together. Molly tells me what's going to happen in the future at school—like which teachers are nice, which ones are mean, and which ones give lots of homework. Then I'll tell Jeff, who's a year younger than me, about my experiences. I'm glad we have each other to depend on for information. It's easier to deal with future changes at school if you're prepared for them.

Sometimes I have to baby-sit for my younger brothers and sisters—Sam, Kelly, Mike, and Anna. They can get pretty wild, especially Mike. He has the sort of personality that influences Anna to act wild, too. And sometimes when I'm in charge, Anna copies me. She'll say "Stop that!" to everyone after I say it. That's funny and pretty cool.

JEFF: ONE OF THE BEST THINGS about being in a big family is that there's always something to do and somebody to do it with. I enjoy playing baseball with my brothers and sisters. Since I'm officially one of the oldest ones living at home permanently, my younger brothers and sisters listen to me. I feel like I have power.

The older kids in my family do their own laundry. I like it that way—a lot! If my mom does it (and she has), my brothers grab all the clean clothes. Then one of them might take a shirt I like a lot. I'll have to let him wear it because my mom thinks we should all try to share.

There's lots of sharing things in a big family—toys, clothes, and books. Sometimes my siblings take things without asking. I don't like that, but it's bound to happen—and I'm used to it.

One super thing about being in a big family is that my younger siblings look up to me. I'm Mike's mentor. He copies me and follows me around. My mentor is Matt. He's twenty-three and getting married soon. Even though we're not blood related, we're a lot alike. My mom says, "You act exactly the way Matt acted when he was your age—all your mannerisms are almost identical." Nobody else in my family is that much like somebody else. I guess Matt kind of rubbed off on me because we've always been so close.

Front row, left to right: ELIZABETH, KATIE, BILL, JEFF;
Middle row, left to right: MATT, MOLLY, DREW (BEHIND MOLLY),
ANNA (SEATED), MIKE (ON SWING); *Top row, left to right:* KELLY, SAM

SAM: ONE OF THE BEST THINGS about being in a big family is there are lots of people to help you with your homework. If I don't know something, I'll ask Elizabeth, Jeff, or Matt. They'll help me. Most other kids don't have that advantage.

Some of my brothers and sisters still live at home. Others are in college or are on their own, but everyone visits a lot. So we eat dinner with lots of people. I never know who might stop in. That's another thing about being in a big family that's lots of fun.

At meals, we have two tables where we eat, the big table and the little table. The big table is for the older kids, and the little table is for the younger ones. We don't have any special age when we can sit at certain tables. It just depends on where there's room and who's at home.

We have seven bedrooms in our house. We use one as a den. Until we're in high school, we each have to share a room. I usually like the company, so getting my own room isn't a big deal. Right now I'm sharing a room with Jeff. He's nice to share with. He's neat and quiet. I used to share with Mike, and he's kind of messy and noisy. But even though he bugged me a lot, he was pretty good company. I don't even know if I'd like sleeping in a room by myself all that much.

I never even think about being an only child. It's more fun having brothers and sisters—and company in my room.

KELLY: I'm never bored or lonely. I always have somebody to talk to or play with.

Even though I have brothers and sisters of all ages, there are some games we can all play together, like the card game Go Fish. A game like that bridges everyone's age, so it's something we can all share. Anna always tries to win, and if she doesn't she might get upset. Because she's the baby, sometimes we let her win. And if we're playing a game the younger kids don't know, they watch us. Then they'll know how to play it when they're a little older.

Anna gets lots of help from all of us, like with learning to ride her bike. My mom sometimes tells us, "Anna doesn't need so many helpers. She needs to learn to do things by herself."

But that's part of being in a big family. You live together and play together and help each other.

MIKE: Usually I like being in a big family. But I do get teased by Jeff, Sam, and Bill. They'll call me names like "wimp." This probably happens because I'm the second youngest kid in the family. I ignore them, and since I know what it's like to get teased, I never tease anyone at school. So growing up in a big family lets me experience situations that have helped me learn how to treat other people.

Most of the things about being in a big family are good. I always have somebody to play with and help me with my homework. Whenever I'm lonely or bored, I can count on Kelly to play with me. And I play a lot with Anna, too.

Playing with Anna makes me feel grown-up and responsible. Let's say we're playing and she leaves her toys on the floor. I'll pick up a toy and she'll copy me. That makes me feel like I'm very grown-up because I'm setting an example for somebody younger. My older brothers and sisters did that for me, and now I can set an example for Anna.

Besides being the second youngest, I have another very special place in the family. I was born on Thanksgiving. So we don't just have Thanksgiving at my house—we have my birthday celebration, too. That's pretty cool.

Holidays are a big deal at my house. My brothers and sisters who don't live at home anymore all visit. The minute they walk in, there's lots of hugging. That's really super. It's fun when all of us are together again.

Klaudia

AGE 10

Some families have parents, grandparents, and other family members all living together.

KLAUDIA: I'M THE ONLY CHILD in a house with lots of adults, so I get lots and lots of attention. I live with my mom, my grandmother, my Uncle Mark, and my cousin David. I love living with all of them—and living in America. I was five when my mother and I moved here from Poland.

My grandmother was living in the United States and told us how nice it was. So my mother and I came to visit. Then we decided to make arrangements to stay here. I love the U.S. There are so many shops with items to buy.

My mother and I are very close. We take lots of trips together. We went to Canada a few weeks ago. Last winter we went to Mexico. One of these days we'll go back to Poland together.

My mother and I go in-line skating together often. She's very good at it. For a few years, we acted in a Polish theater group together. My mother does more things with me than most mothers do with their kids, so I'm very fortunate.

I'm also very close to my grandmother. She doesn't go on trips with my mother and me. She's afraid to fly. She doesn't skate, either. My grandmother loves to cook, and I like to help her with the cooking. Last night we made blueberry kolachkies. Kolachkies are filled cookies that are very popular in Poland. On Sundays, I almost always help her cook the meal. That's a special day for us. My mom, cousin, uncle, grandmother, and I all have dinner together.

My cousin David, who is eighteen, is also very special to me. He's like a big brother. He drives me to my ballet and acrobat lessons. At my last birthday party, he helped out. He even packed the goody bags. He skates, too. Sometimes he comes with my mom and me. Once in a while he'll take me skating with his friends.

My Uncle Mark is my godfather. He hasn't lived in this country very long, and he might not stay here. He doesn't like America as much as the rest of us do. I hope he learns to like it. I enjoy all of us being here together.

Left to right: KLAUDIA, ELIZABETH (MOM), ANNA (GRANDMOTHER), DAVID (COUSIN)

Maria and Emmanuel

AGE 10

Some families have relatives who live nearby.

| MARIA: | BESIDES BEING MY COUSIN, Emmanuel is a good friend. We have a very good relationship. |

We live in the same apartment building and are in the same room at school, so we see lots of each other. It's almost like we're sister and brother. We even look a little alike. So sometimes I pretend that we're sister and brother.

Emmanuel and I are so close that he helps me out. Last year I broke my arm and had a cast on it. Emmanuel came over every day to help me do my chores around the house.

Emmanuel and I play together after school and on weekends. We play soccer and football at the park. In the winter, we make snowmen. In the summer, we go to the beach and build sand castles with Emmanuel's sister Daisy.

I have a brother who is a year older than me. His name is Geraldo. He goes to a special school because he has a hearing

Special thanks to Steve Brown, bilingual teacher at Gale School in Chicago, for interpreting the interview with Maria and Emmanuel, who speak both Spanish and English.

impairment. But Emmanuel and I can still communicate with him through sign language. Some of it is real sign language, and some of it contains signs that only Emmanuel and I do with him. Sometimes Geraldo plays sports with us, too.

This summer, Emmanuel will go to Mexico for a month. I'll miss him. I'll write to

Left to right: DAISY (EMMANUEL'S SISTER), EMMANUEL, MARIA

him and he'll write to me. I'll think about what he's doing while he's gone. Maybe someday we can all visit Mexico together.

EMMANUEL: I LIKE HAVING A COUSIN my age living so close to me. Because I see Maria so much, it's like having a sister the same age as I am. So I always have somebody to play with and talk to. Sometimes I pretend we're brother and sister. So, in a way, I have two sisters—Maria, my cousin, and Daisy, my real sister, who is eight years old.

It's nice having Maria in the same class, because when one of us is out of school, we can bring each other our homework. Sometimes we do our homework together and help each other. That makes the homework easier and kind of fun to do.

Maria and I like to play soccer, football, and tennis outside. Inside, we play Candyland or Guess Who with Daisy.

Sometimes Maria and I talk to each other in English, and sometimes we talk in Spanish. And sometimes we use the special sign language that we use for communicating with Geraldo.

In May, our parents have a party for Cinco de Mayo—that's a day to celebrate our Mexican heritage. We listen to Mexican music on the stereo and dance. We eat tamales, beans, and tacos. On the Mexican Day of the Dead, which happens in November, we put out pictures of our relatives who have passed away. It gives us a chance to think about our ancestors. I wonder about the relatives I never met and what they were like. It's great having somebody my own age to experience important Mexican holidays with.

I'll be going to Mexico very soon to visit my grandmother and grandfather. I'm looking forward to the visit, but I'll miss Maria. I'll write to her and bring her a present—maybe a pair of Mexican sandals. And while I'm there I'll wish we were together.

Front row, left to right: GANZALO (EMMANUEL'S DAD), LUISSA (EMMANUEL'S MOM), DAISY (EMMANUEL'S SISTER), MARIA; *Top row, left to right:* EMMANUEL, GERALDO (MARIA'S BROTHER)

You and Your Family

Family History

How to make a family tree and family history scrapbook.

IT'S FUN TO DISCOVER facts about past and present relatives. You can collect this information about your family, then share it by making a family tree. Even if you don't live with your biological family, you can still enjoy finding out about family members. You'll probably learn that you have lots of things in common.

As you research your family, you'll discover interesting information about your relatives and yourself. Maybe you have artistic talent, like your great-grandfather did. Maybe you have a way with animals, like your great-great-grandmother did. You could be related to someone famous or somebody with an occupation similar to one you're considering for your future career.

Making a Family Tree

A family tree is a chart that lists your ancestors and gives information about them. Most family trees include *direct-line relatives*—parents, grandparents, and great-grandparents. Some charts go back farther than that. Another name for a direct-line family tree is a *pedigree chart*.

Family trees usually include the following information for each person (or as much of it as you can find):

- full name (last name first)
- date and place of birth
- date and place of marriage (each woman is listed by her maiden name—the name she had before she was married, if she changed it when she married)
- date and place of death.

Since you'll be recording important information about your family members, you'll need a notebook especially for this purpose. A loose-leaf or spiral notebook is perfect. Use a separate page for each family member. That way, you'll have room to write down all the information you discover.

On the next two pages, you'll find an example of a real family tree chart.

Matthew Erlbach's

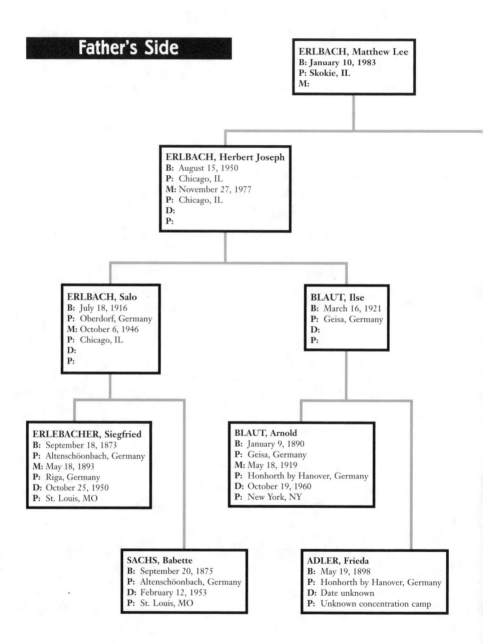

ERLBACH, Matthew Lee
B: January 10, 1983
P: Skokie, IL
M:

ERLBACH, Herbert Joseph
B: August 15, 1950
P: Chicago, IL
M: November 27, 1977
P: Chicago, IL
D:
P:

ERLBACH, Salo
B: July 18, 1916
P: Oberdorf, Germany
M: October 6, 1946
P: Chicago, IL
D:
P:

BLAUT, Ilse
B: March 16, 1921
P: Geisa, Germany
D:
P:

ERLEBACHER, Siegfried
B: September 18, 1873
P: Altenschöonbach, Germany
M: May 18, 1893
P: Riga, Germany
D: October 25, 1950
P: St. Louis, MO

BLAUT, Arnold
B: January 9, 1890
P: Geisa, Germany
M: May 18, 1919
P: Honhorth by Hanover, Germany
D: October 19, 1960
P: New York, NY

SACHS, Babette
B: September 20, 1875
P: Altenschöonbach, Germany
D: February 12, 1953
P: St. Louis, MO

ADLER, Frieda
B: May 19, 1898
P: Honhorth by Hanover, Germany
D: Date unknown
P: Unknown concentration camp

Family Tree

B = Born **M = Married**
P = Place **D = Died**

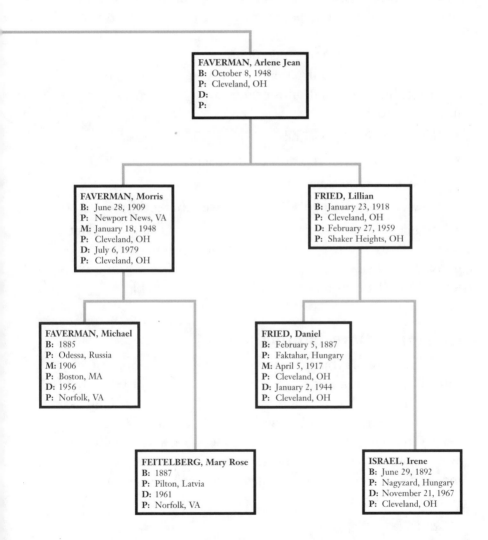

FAVERMAN, Arlene Jean
B: October 8, 1948
P: Cleveland, OH
D:
P:

FAVERMAN, Morris
B: June 28, 1909
P: Newport News, VA
M: January 18, 1948
P: Cleveland, OH
D: July 6, 1979
P: Cleveland, OH

FRIED, Lillian
B: January 23, 1918
P: Cleveland, OH
D: February 27, 1959
P: Shaker Heights, OH

FAVERMAN, Michael
B: 1885
P: Odessa, Russia
M: 1906
P: Boston, MA
D: 1956
P: Norfolk, VA

FRIED, Daniel
B: February 5, 1887
P: Faktahar, Hungary
M: April 5, 1917
P: Cleveland, OH
D: January 2, 1944
P: Cleveland, OH

FEITELBERG, Mary Rose
B: 1887
P: Pilton, Latvia
D: 1961
P: Norfolk, VA

ISRAEL, Irene
B: June 29, 1892
P: Nagyzard, Hungary
D: November 21, 1967
P: Cleveland, OH

Getting Started: Finding Out about Your Immediate Family

Your family tree begins with you. You're the first generation, or branch, on your family tree. So write down information about yourself first. Some of the types of information listed on page 63 won't apply yet, of course, like your marriage date. But you'll need to record your date and place of birth. Leave room for a marriage date; if you save your family tree, you can fill this out years from now if and when you do get married. Include your brothers' and sisters' information, too. They're on the same branch as you, since you're all from the same generation.

Next, interview your parents, then your grandparents. As you collect information for your family tree, ask questions like these, too:

• What are your special talents?

• What subjects did you do well in at school?

• What type of jobs have you had?

• How are you and I alike? How are we different?

You won't need this information to make your family tree, but these facts are fun to know. They will help you to understand more about yourself and your family members. You can use this information later to make a family history scrapbook.

Gathering More Information

Finding out about your immediate family (parents and siblings) should be easy. You just need to ask. Learning about your grandparents may be easy, too. But the farther back you move in your family research, the harder it will be to obtain the information you need. Great-grandparents and other ancestors have usually passed away. Most of the people who knew them may have passed away, too. You may need to do some detective work to discover what you'd like to know.

Elderly family members, like great-aunts and older cousins, may be able to answer your questions about people from past generations. If any older relatives live near you, interview them, too. Visit them and show them your notebook. This may help to jog their memories.

Some relatives may not live near you, so you won't be able to interview them face-to-face. You can still get in touch with them easily by:

- writing a letter. (TIP: Send a self-addressed, stamped envelope when requesting information. This makes it easier for people to reply to you.)
- sending E-mail. (Both you and your relative must have a computer and a modem)
- phoning when rates are low. (Make sure you have your parents' permission.)

Your letter or E-mail might look like this:

Dear Cousin Albert,

I'm making a family tree and would like information on my great-grandmother, Helen Jones Walker. I understand you were very close to her. Could you send me the following information, if you know it:

— her date and place of birth
— her date of marriage
— her date and place of death.

Thank you for your help!

Yours truly,
Ellen Walker

Other possible sources of information about family members include family Bibles, prayer books, photo albums, and scrapbooks. Your parents might have kept their own baby books or scrapbooks from high school and college. Leaf through them. You may find some facts you can add to your notebook or use to complete your family tree.

Obtaining Hard-to-Find Information

You may live with one parent and only have contact with his or her family. In that case, try your best to research the other side of your family. If the research will cause hard feelings for any reason, leave that branch out for now. Researching your family tree is supposed to be fun for everyone.

Sometimes, no matter how hard you try, you won't be able to obtain the information you need from relatives. You might need to use other sources. Here are some suggestions.

Public Libraries

Many public libraries have special *genealogy* sections. (Genealogy is the investigation or study of ancestry and family history.) These sections contain newspaper clippings and records about people who have lived in the area. If a relative you'd like to find out about lived in an area near you, visit that library and use its genealogy section. Ask the librarian for help. If the relative didn't live nearby, you may still be able to find out about him or her. Your local library may be able to help you by ordering information from that relative's town. You'll need to know where that relative lived and the approximate dates of his or her birth and death.

Historical Societies

Sometimes town, city, and state historical societies offer the same types of information as libraries. There are directories of historical societies and their addresses available in many libraries. You may be able to write to a historical society and find the information that you need.

Branch Genealogical Libraries
of the Mormon Church

The Mormon Church owns the largest collection of genealogical records in the world. You don't need to be a Mormon or have a Mormon in your family to use the collection.

There are almost 500 branch genealogical libraries in the world. They won't answer mailed inquiries about relatives; you must go into a library in person to use it. To find out the location of the branch genealogical library nearest you, look under "Churches" in the Yellow Pages, then look under "Church of Jesus Christ of the Latter-day Saints."

If there is no Mormon church in your area, write to: Branch Genealogical Libraries, The Genealogical Society, 50 East North Temple Street, Salt Lake City, UT 84150. Ask for the address of the branch genealogical library closest to where you live. Depending on how far away it is, maybe you and your family can take a short trip together for this purpose. Be sure to call ahead to find out the days and hours the library is open.

Your letter might look like this:

```
To Whom It May Concern:

I am interested in doing a genealogical ·search for
my family, and I would like to use one of your
branch genealogical libraries. There is no Mormon
church in my area. Could you send me information
about the branch genealogical library closest to
me? I live in [name of your town or city and
state]. I will need to know the address and tele-
phone number of the library. I am enclosing a
self-addressed, stamped business-size
envelope for your reply. Thank you for your help.

Sincerely,
Thomas Ames
```

Public Records

If you know where a person was born or where he or she died, you may be able to obtain his or her birth and death dates by writing to the county courthouse in the town where the person lived. You can find out more about obtaining these records by ordering a pamphlet from the United States Department of Health and Human Services. Write to: Consumer Information, Center—2, P.O. Box 100, Pueblo, CO 81002 and request the pamphlet called "Where to Write for Vital Records."

Recording Your Information

Once you've collected your family's information, you'll want to share it with other family members and friends. Here are some ideas for how to display the information you've discovered.

The Pedigree Chart

Some people write their family's information on a graph called a pedigree chart. A pedigree chart follows a certain format. You can copy and use the pedigree chart on pages 100–101 of this book, or you can make your own. On page 99, you'll find instructions for how to fill in your chart.

Tree Displays

You can display your information in tree form by drawing a tree on a large piece of paper or poster board. Draw leaves, circles, squares, or other shapes with room for writing. Fill in each family member's information. Or you can cut leaves or shapes from construction paper and paste them onto the tree's branches.

You can even make a three-dimensional family tree by cutting your tree from heavy cardboard. Then insert the bottom into a block of Styrofoam so it will stand.

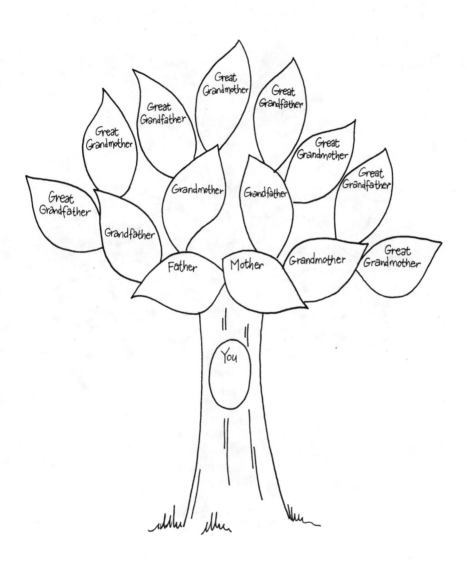

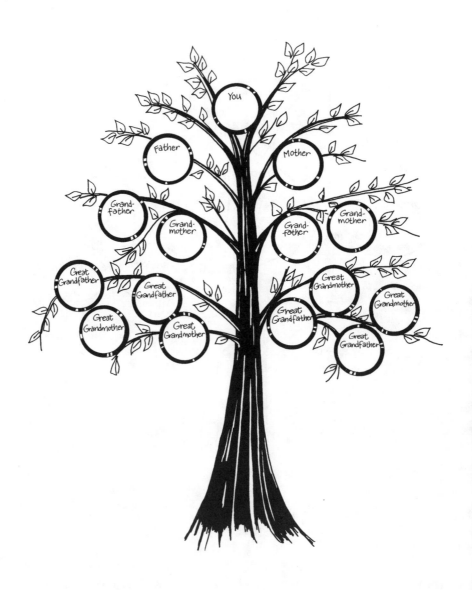

More Ways to Display Family Facts

There are many other ways to present your family's information besides a basic pedigree chart or family tree. Here are some ideas to get you started:

- If you have a last name like Lambert, Fisher, or Katz, make lamb, fish, or cat cutouts to record each ancestor's information. Then attach the cutouts to cardboard. (Our last name, "Erlbach," means "a type of stream." A few years ago, our son Matthew made a family tree with each name on a fish cutout.)

- Find out if your last name has a special meaning or translation. For example, Tannenbaum means "Christmas tree" in German. Rosa means "rose" in Italian. Yamashita means "one who lives near a mountain" in Japanese. Use symbols instead of leaves for your family chart.

- If your family is from all over the United States or the world, mount your information on a map.

- Add photographs of family members to your pedigree chart or family tree. Or add a few sentences telling about each family member's interests and talents. The whole point is to design your family chart so it's meaningful to you and your family.

Making a Family History Scrapbook

While researching your family tree, you'll learn a lot about your family members. You'll discover something unique or special about each person.

Maybe you'll dig up your parents' old report cards, class pictures, and photographs of them when they were the same age you are now. You may find their awards from school or camp. Collect this memorabilia and put it into a family history scrapbook. You can buy a scrapbook at a discount drugstore or department store. Or you can make your own scrapbook by binding heavy construction paper together with fasteners.

Include a few pages about each family member in your family scrapbook. Leave some pages blank so you can add memorabilia about future events as they happen. Keep your family history scrapbook in a safe place. One day you may want to show it to your nieces, nephews, younger cousins—or your own children.

Family Memories and Keepsakes

Fun ways to preserve special moments in your family history.

BESIDES FAMILY TREES and family history scrapbooks, you can create family timelines, quilts, photo sculptures, shadow boxes, and time capsules to preserve family memories. Here are some ideas for fun things to make for yourself or to give as gifts to other family members.

Making a Family Timeline

You've probably seen timelines in history books at school. Time-lines are charts that list important events in history and the dates when they occurred. Your family has a history with important dates, too, like:

- the day your parents met or got married
- the day you or one of your siblings was born or adopted
- the day your family moved to your house or apartment
- the day you brought home a pet
- the day you came home from camp with your Super Swimmer award.

  Here's what you'll need for your family timeline:
- writing paper
- a pencil

- several sheets of plain (unlined) white paper or continuous-feed computer paper
- tape (if you don't have continuous-feed computer paper, you'll need to attach the separate sheets)
- markers and crayons
- glue
- photographs and/or souvenirs of important family events.

Here's how to make your timeline:

1. Make a list of important family events and their dates. If nobody remembers the exact date of a particular event, just the year will do. It doesn't matter what order you list them in.

2. Now write down each event and its date on a separate sheet of paper. You may want to describe the event, too. What do you remember about it? What do other family members recall? Did anything funny or important happen? Try to think of a few interesting details to include.

3. Illustrate each event with photographs or pictures you draw. If you have any souvenirs, like a brochure from a vacation your family took together, glue these to your timeline.

4. Arrange the sheets in chronological order and attach them with tape. Add new events to your timeline as they happen.

The Alvarez Family Timeline

Making a Family Quilt

A family quilt displays interesting facts about your family through pictures. You don't need to know how to sew to make your family quilt. All you need to do is draw or make paper cutouts.

Here's what you'll need for your family quilt:

- several squares of paper measuring 6" x 6" (the number depends on how many facts and events you want to show in your quilt)
- a large sheet of cardboard or poster board
- glue
- markers, crayons, and/or colored paper
- scissors.

Here's how to make your family quilt:

1. Make a list of family facts and events you would like to include in your quilt. If you want to include nine facts or events, you'll need nine squares of 6" x 6" paper. If you want to include 12 facts or events, you'll need 12 squares.

2. Each square on your quilt will be a picture of somebody or something important to you and your family. Does your brother play the piano? Draw a picture of him surrounded by musical notes. Do you have an aquarium? Paste fish on one of the squares. Did you go on a vacation last year? Include a drawing about that, too.

3. If you want, you can have your siblings and parents design squares for the quilt. Then have each person sign and date his or her square.

4. Glue the squares onto the cardboard or poster board. If possible, you may want to laminate your quilt so the entire family can enjoy it for a long time. It might even become a family heirloom.

Turn the page to see an example of a family quilt.

TEACHERS: A family quilt is a good classroom project. Each child draws or cuts out pictures about his or her family, then everyone mounts their squares on a huge sheet of tagboard. I did this with my students and hung the quilt outside my room for open house. Everyone—kids and parents—loved it.

Making a Family Photo Sculpture

Most family members have pictures or portraits taken of them, either individually or as a family. You can make your family's pictures special by designing a three-dimensional photo sculpture. All you need to do is mount your family's photographs and stand them up.

A family photo sculpture is a super gift for your mom or dad—or to give to a sibling who'll be leaving for college.

Here's what you'll need for your family photo sculpture:

- photographs of family members (either group photos or pictures of each family member; full-body pictures of people standing work best)
- poster board or shirt cardboard
- glue
- scissors
- a block of Styrofoam
- craft sticks (available at art supplies stores, these are just like Popsicle sticks—of course, you can also save and use Popsicle sticks)
- poster paints.

Here's how to make your family photo sculpture:

1. Select photographs from your family photo album. (TIP: If you're going to be using pictures from photo albums, make sure it's okay with your folks. If they have the negatives, you can make duplicates—and even have the photographs enlarged.)

2. If you can't find photographs you want to use, take your own pictures or have somebody take them for you. This doesn't need to be a professional photographer—just someone you know who takes good, sharp pictures.

Photos glued to cardboard, cut out, glued to craft sticks

Craft sticks

Styrofoam block

3. Once you have your photographs, glue each one onto the tag-board or shirt cardboard. Then cut around the people to remove the background.

4. Glue the cut-out photographs to craft sticks.

5. Push your mounted photographs into the block of Styrofoam.

6. Paint the Styrofoam, if you want.

Making a Family Shadow Box

A family shadow box contains photo sculptures plus family memorabilia. Your shadow box can focus on a special family event, like a vacation, first communion, bar mitzvah, or graduation.

A family shadow box makes a great gift for a parent's important birthday—like when your mom or dad turns 30, 40, or 50.
A shadow box also makes a terrific Mother's Day or Father's Day present.

Here's what you'll need for your shadow box:

- an empty shoe box

- individual photo sculptures (or a group photo sculpture) mounted on small blocks of Styrofoam

- photographs or drawings of your home, vacation, or anything else you'd like to include (examples: a graduation program,

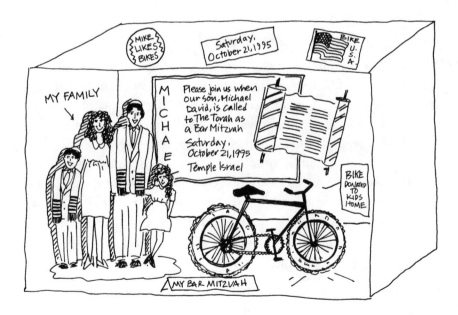

tickets to your dance recital, a brochure from a family vacation, or memorabilia from other special events)

- miniature toys, objects, figures, or other fun things that remind you of a special event
- poster paints
- clear plastic wrap
- glue.

Here's how to make your family shadow box:

1. Paint your shoe box inside and out.
2. Decorate the background with memorabilia.
3. When you're done decorating your shoe box, glue in the photo sculptures and anything else you want to include in your shadow box.
4. Cover the front with clear plastic wrap.
5. Display your shadow box where your whole family can enjoy it.

Making a Family Time Capsule

A time capsule contains items that represent a certain date or period of time. Once the items are selected and put in the capsule, the capsule is buried in the ground. People dig it up later to find out how things were when it was buried. Some time capsules stay buried for hundreds or thousands of years.

You can make a family time capsule and dig it up in a year or two. (Of course, you can also store your family time capsule in a special place instead of burying it. Try a high closet shelf, a corner of the attic or basement, or under your bed!)

Here's what you'll need for your family time capsule:

- a metal box or plastic freezer bag
- a slip of paper or 3" x 5" card showing the date and time you are burying your time capsule

- a Polaroid picture of your family taken on that day
- a Polaroid picture of your pet(s) taken on that day
- a newspaper from that day.

  You'll also want to include information about your family. Here are some suggestions:

- a list of everyone's favorite food that day—or what they ate for every meal
- a list of what you laughed and argued about on that day
- a description of something important or funny each family member did that day
- a list of movies and songs that were popular on that day.

  You might also want to ask each family member to write a secret wish, dream, or hope to include in the time capsule. Have them use separate pieces of paper, put them in envelopes, and seal the envelopes so no one else can see what they wrote until the time capsule is opened again.

  Here's what to do with your family time capsule:

1. Gather everything you want to include in your time capsule.
2. Carefully put everything into a metal box or a freezer bag. Close the box or seal the bag.
3. Bury your time capsule. Or, if you don't have a place to bury it, put it in a special place.
4. If you have a calendar that shows next year and the year after, mark it to show the date (a year from now? two years from now?) when you want to dig up or take out your time capsule.
5. When that date comes, call your family together and open your family time capsule. Compare the data in the capsule to the way your family is on that day. Then make another time capsule.

Family Traditions

Special things families do together.

TRADITIONS ARE IMPORTANT activities that families do at specific times, like holidays, special occasions, or even on certain days of the week. Maybe your family always uses a special plate for serving birthday cakes. Or perhaps your family celebrates holidays at a certain relative's home. Maybe you eat at a favorite restaurant when one of the kids in your family gets a super report card. These are your family's traditions.

Traditions remind you of how special and unique your family is. They give you warm family feelings. They help you feel closer to family members.

Types of Family Traditions

Many family traditions are religious or ethnic. They remind people that they're members of a certain religious or ethnic group. Traditions are attached to holidays or important life events, like birthdays and weddings. Most people who belong to a particular ethnic or religious group practice that group's traditions, not just individual families. If your family is Scandinavian, for example, celebrating St. Lucia's Day on December 13 is a Christmas season tradition. Having a Bar or Bat Mitzvah when you're twelve or thirteen is a special birthday tradition if you're Jewish.

Other family traditions may be practiced by your family only. Some traditions may be generations old. Maybe for each Memorial Day your family displays the American flag that belonged to your great-grandfather. Maybe you have a party on your dog's birthday or collect clothes for a children's home once a year. Traditions can be serious, sentimental, or humorous.

Following are descriptions of traditions common to many families.

Birthday Traditions

Birthdays are important events in most families. Each person's birthday is his or her own special holiday. Some families and ethnic groups treat certain birthdays as turning points in a person's life, so these birthdays are treated as special events. Other families have certain things they do every year on family members' birthdays, or they have a special ceremony when a new family member is born.

- Fifteen-year-old Hispanic girls often have Quinciñeras. A Quinciñera is an elaborate party, almost like a wedding, that presents a young girl to society. Long ago, the event signified that the girl was ready for marriage. Now it often means that she is old enough to date.

- Lots of American kids have a special birthday party when they turn 16. If you live in a state where 16 is the legal driving age, your parents may take you for your driver's test to celebrate.

- Jewish girls have a Bat Mitzvah when they're 12. Boys have a Bar Mitzvah when they're 13. A Bat or Bar Mitzvah means a child has become a religious adult. A special service happens at a synagogue with a party afterward.

- Some Native American tribes have a special monthly birthday celebration in their tribal hall. Everybody who has a birthday that month celebrates together. The party includes children and adults.

- Many families keep a birthday scrapbook for each child. They save invitations, photographs, favors, and even the wrapping paper from some of the gifts.

- Some families have a permanent decoration or candle that they use on birthday cakes.

- Some African Americans lift their infant children up to the sky when a child is born. This shows that there is nothing greater than a newborn child.

Holiday Traditions

Every family has its own special way of celebrating holidays. Some holiday traditions are ethnic. Some are religious. Some are just plain holiday traditions. You may want to try some of these traditions with your family.

- In the southern United States, some families eat Hopping John—a mixture of beans and rice—on New Year's Day for good luck.

- Some families don't purchase a separate Christmas gift for each member. Instead, everyone secretly draws a family member's name out of a hat. Then they make or buy something for that person.

- Pets are part of many families' holiday celebrations. A dog might receive a Christmas or Hanukkah bone. A cat might get sardines. Some people tie colored ribbons on their pets' collars that represent various holidays.

- After Halloween, some families toast the seeds from their jack-o-lanterns and eat them.

- Some Mexican families have a special feast honoring the dead on the first three days of November.

- Some families have grab-bags at Thanksgiving. These aren't grab-bags for gifts. Instead, everyone picks a card describing a chore they'll do, like make the salad, set the table, or clean up.

One person gets a "freebie" card and doesn't have to do anything but sit and wait for the meal to be served.

- Some families have Secret Santas during December. Each family member chooses another by drawing a name out of a hat. Then the family member acts as that person's Secret Santa, giving him or her little gifts and maybe secretly doing his or her chores for the month.

- Some families invite one or two people they know will be alone to join them for a holiday dinner. This might be an elderly neighbor whose family lives far away, or somebody who has just moved into town.

- Some Polish people get their food blessed before Easter.

- During the month of Ramadan, Muslims eat nothing between sunrise and sundown. When Ramadan ends, families gather for a feast.

- Jewish people celebrate a special New Year during the fall. It's customary for them to eat apples and honey to signify a sweet upcoming year.

Personal Family Traditions

Almost every family does something that's special to them. The tradition may be something the family has just decided to do, or something that family has done for generations.

- Some families have a special Saturday or Sunday each month when they visit a museum together.

- Some families volunteer together to help others. They have a project they're all involved in—like working at a homeless shelter once a month, or collecting money for a certain charity.

- If a family has members with musical talents, they might have a family talent night. Each family member sings a song, dances, or plays an instrument for the rest of the family.

- Some families have a certain time each night when the entire family reads. The reading material doesn't have to be a serious book or a classic. It can be anything a family member chooses, even a magazine or comic book.

- Many families have a change jar that they put all their extra change into. When it's filled, the family goes out to dinner together or buys something that everyone can use.

- Some families adopt an animal at their local zoo. This doesn't mean that they take the animal home. Instead, they pay a small fee, and afterward they receive a photograph and newsletters about their animal. They visit the zoo and take pictures outside their adopted animal's cage or living area.

- Most families have picnics outside when the weather is warm. Some have them on rainy or snowy days, too. They put a picnic blanket in the family room or kitchen and have their picnic inside the house.

Starting Your Own Family Traditions

Your family probably already practices its own traditions. This doesn't mean that you can't start new traditions of your own. Think about the things your family likes. Movies? Animals? Gardening? Make up some special activities related to those things that you can do regularly with family members. Here are some ideas to get you started:

- Offer to make dinner one day a month. The adults don't do any work at all. You and your brothers and sisters take care of everything, from planning the meal to cleaning up afterward. If you're an only child, you do everything by yourself.

- Plant a vegetable garden together in the spring. When the growing season is over, harvest your vegetables and make vegetable soup. Freeze it and serve it on a special day a few months later.

- Have a role-playing night. Have each member sit at a different place during dinner and imitate the person who usually sits there. This means acting really silly. Slurp your soup if your little sister does—or ask how your parents did on their spelling test or book report, if that's something they usually ask you about.

- Do your brothers or sisters wear braces on their teeth? Take a picture of what they look like in braces. When the braces come off, take more pictures. Then serve them everything they couldn't eat when they wore braces, like taffy apples and chewing gum. (If you're the one who wears braces, start this tradition with you.)

- Have an "unbirthday party" once a year. Pick a date. Bake or buy a cake with everyone's name on it. Light lots of candles and blow them out together. Have a grab-bag of inexpensive gifts.

- Have a family volunteer day. Offer to help a family member with a chore he or she hates to do.

- Have a video weekend once a month. Everyone chooses a video and the family watches it together. You can even write reviews and make popcorn.

- Make a family newspaper once a month. Have everyone write something interesting about another family member. Then make copies and pass them out to everyone in the family. If your immediate family is small, include information about aunts, uncles, grandparents, and cousins.

- Have a dinner where everyone eats his or her favorite food—no matter what it is. If your favorite food is chocolate cake, your sister's is gumdrops, your mom's is ice cream, and your dad's is lemon squares, then that's the dinner. (The favorite food dinner may not be very nutritious, so this tradition is something to practice only occasionally.)

Family Meetings

Ways to settle family problems and make family decisions.

No FAMILY CAN LIVE together 365 days a year without getting on each other's nerves from time to time. Maybe you share your room with a sloppy, pesky, or bossy sibling. Maybe one of your parents has remarried. You like your stepparent, but you wish that he or she wouldn't try so hard to take your biological parent's place. Or maybe a parent embarrasses you without realizing it. Your mom asks your friends nosy questions or calls you names like "Lambkin" in public.

Maybe you try to talk things over privately with the offender, but it doesn't seem to work. A good way to settle problems and make other family decisions is at a family meeting.

When and How to Call a Family Meeting

Tell your family that you'd like to have a family meeting. Explain that there is a problem you want to talk over with them. Say that they will have the chance to talk, too. The meeting won't just be for and about you.

Set a specific time and date for the meeting. Be fair. If your gripe is about your little sister who always borrows your clothes, don't schedule the meeting for when she's at soccer practice or Girl Scouts. Everyone needs to be there, including the offender.

Make sure the meeting is at a time when everyone is relaxed and alert. Don't plan or call a meeting the minute your mom arrives home from a business trip, or when your parents are wall-papering the den.

How to Conduct a Family Meeting

Start the meeting by thanking everyone for coming. Explain that this meeting has a special purpose: to give everyone a chance to talk about a problem they are having with the family. If this is your first family meeting, say that you would like to go first so you can demonstrate the process. Then follow these steps:

1. State the *main* problem you are having with a certain family member. Stick to the facts and don't exaggerate. For example, you might say, "Alicia borrows my clothes without asking. She does this almost every day. Yesterday I needed my blue shirt for school, but I couldn't find it anywhere. She was wearing it at breakfast. I don't mind loaning her some of my clothes some of the time, but I really want her to ask before she takes them."

   Don't go on and on about everything that bugs you about that family member. This is *not* the time to mention that you hate the way Alicia combs her hair and the way she chews her food.

2. Let the person you're complaining about tell his or her side of the situation. Often, problems are caused or made worse by the way two or more people interact with each other. Listen respectfully while the other person is talking.

3. Invite other family members to offer suggestions about how to solve your problem. You and the person you're griping about may be too emotionally involved to come to a realistic solution.

4. Agree to try some of the suggestions. Set a date for a family meeting in the future to discuss your progress. If the suggestions don't work by then, you can agree to try something else.

   If your family has had meetings before, don't automatically go first, even if you are the one who called the meeting. Give everyone an equal chance to speak first. Draw straws or numbers. The person with the highest number or longest straw gets to start the meeting.

When Family Problems Are Very Difficult

Sometimes family problems are too big or too complex to solve at a family meeting or even discuss with family members. In cases like these, you need outside help. You may want to suggest that your family visit a counselor together. If this is not possible for whatever reason, discuss your problems with your minister, priest, rabbi, school social worker, school psychologist, or school counselor. Don't give up until you find an adult you trust who will listen to you. You *will* find someone.

If you need help *immediately*—if you are in danger or feel desperate—look under "Crisis Intervention Services" in the Yellow Pages and find a number to call. Some phone books list a Crisis Intervention phone number on the inside front cover. Or you can call one of these national crisis hotlines:

Child Help National Child Abuse Hotline
1-800-422-4453

Boys Town National Hotline
1-800-448-3000
1-800-448-1833 (hearing impaired)

For more information about dealing with family problems, you may want to read one or more of the books listed below. Ask your librarian for other recommendations.

- *Dysfunctional Families* by Valerie Lee Lynch (Vero Beach, FL: The Rourke Corporation, Inc., 1990).
- *Everything You Need to Know about Family Violence* by Evan Stark (New York: The Rosen Publishing Group, 1995).
- *Everything You Need to Know about Stepfamilies* by Bruce Glassman (New York: The Rosen Publishing Group, 1994).
- *Living With a Single Parent* by Maxine B. Rosenberg (New York: Bradbury Press, 1992).
- *Something's Wrong in My House* by Katherine Leiner (New York: Franklin Watts, 1988).

Extended Family

Family is more than the people you live with.

So far, we've talked mostly about immediate family—the people you live with. Most kids have extended family, too—aunts, uncles, cousins, grandparents. Sometimes a family has honorary relatives—people who aren't related but are such good family friends that you call them Aunt, Uncle, or Cousin.

If your extended family lives nearby, you may see these people often. Your grandparents may visit regularly. Your aunts, uncles, and cousins may pop in often and sometimes unexpectedly. You and/or your parents may chat with relatives over the phone every day or every week. You may be so used to your extended family that they seem almost as close as your immediate family.

Who's Who in the Family: A Guide for When It Gets Confusing

Sometimes it's confusing to know who all of your relatives really are. For example, there may be someone in your family you call Aunt or Uncle because she or he is older than you. But that person isn't your aunt or uncle at all. She or he is really your mom or dad's *first cousin*. Or maybe you have some people in your family you call Aunt or Uncle—and so does your mother or father. These are your *great-aunts* and *great-uncles*.

If you want to know who's who in your family and how each person is related to you, here's help:

- Your parents' parents are your *grandparents*. If one of your grandparents divorced and remarried, you may have stepgrandparents, too.
- Your parents' grandparents are your *great-great-grandparents*.
- Your parents' great-grandparents are your *second great-grandparents*—and so on.
- Your mother's brothers and sisters are your *uncles* and *aunts*. If they are married, their spouses are also your uncles and aunts. You are their *niece* or *nephew*.
- Your parents' aunts and uncles are your *great-aunts* and *great-uncles*. You are their *grand-niece* or *grand-nephew*.
- If your siblings marry, their spouses are your *brothers-in-law* or *sisters-in-law*. If they have children, the children are your *nieces* or *nephews*, and you're their *aunt* or *uncle*.
- The children of your aunts and uncles are your *first cousins*.
- The children of your parents' first cousins are your *second cousins*.
- If your first cousins have children, the children are your *first cousins once removed*.
- The children of your second cousins are your *second cousins once removed*.

Spending Time with Favorite Relatives

Your extended family members may live far away in another town or state. If that's the case, you may see them only occasionally at special family gatherings, like holiday celebrations, weddings, or family reunions.

These family gatherings are usually fun. They give you a chance to see favorite relatives. Sometimes you have to deal with relatives you don't like very much—the kinds who ask nosy questions and give you wet kisses. But it's great to see everyone again, eat together, and share family gossip. When the gathering is over, there will be people you'll miss and maybe a few you'll be glad to get away from.

Is there a family gathering in your future? Will a favorite cousin, aunt, or uncle be there—one you would like to spend time with one-on-one? Maybe you've tried to do this at past gatherings, but there's been so much going on that you've barely spent any time with that person. Here are some ways to arrange for more time together:

- Before the gathering, contact the relative by phone or write a letter. Say that you'd like to spend some time with him or her at the gathering. The relative will probably be flattered.

- Suggest something to do together, like playing ball or just chatting. If you're going to a gathering that may last a few days, like a holiday weekend or reunion, suggest going shopping or out for ice cream together.

- Make arrangements to call or write to each other in the future.

If a particular relative is everyone's favorite, be fair. Let other people spend time with him or her, too.

Dealing with Annoying Relatives

Some relatives don't seem to understand that kids have feelings. They ask nosy questions like "Do you wear a bra?" or "Have you been kissed yet?" or "Do you still sleep with the blue bunny I sent you six years ago?" How embarrassing!

If anyone asks you a question you don't want to answer, just say, "I'd rather not discuss it," in a polite voice. You have the right to not answer questions you don't feel comfortable answering. You also have the right not to be kissed by wet kissers or hugged by people who squeeze like boa constrictors.

What should you do if one of your relatives keeps annoying you? See if another relative will agree to rescue you—as in "Sorry to interrupt, Uncle Bill, but it's time to take Pedro swimming!" Or tell your parents about the problem and ask for their help. Maybe they will agree to talk to the offending family member, or maybe they will have other suggestions for you to try.

Staying Close to Faraway Relatives

You may have favorite relatives who live out of town. You wish they lived closer so you could maintain a regular relationship. But because they live so far away, you only get to see them sometimes.

Often, this happens with cousins around the same age. If your favorite cousin lived nearby, you'd hang out together a lot. You'd almost be best friends. Of course, this can also happen with aunts, uncles, and grandparents, or siblings who are older than you and have moved away from home.

Even though you live far from favorite relatives, and even though you can't see each other very often, you can still be close. Following are some ideas for communicating with special family members.

Long-Distance Phone Calls

Long-distance phone calls aren't terribly expensive on weekends or late at night. Set a time when you'll call that favorite relative. (Check with your parents first. Also, it's a good idea to make a brief preliminary phone call or write a postcard to arrange a time.) During your conversation, share what's been going on in your life and with family members who live with you and near you. If your favorite relative lives far away from the rest of the family, he or she will appreciate being filled in on family happenings.

Letters

Everyone loves to receive letters and cards. Write to your favorite relatives regularly, and when they write to you, respond quickly— within the month. Tell them what's happening with you and other family members. Send photographs of family events your favorite relatives weren't able to attend because they live so far away. Send them cards on their birthdays and on holidays. And if there's no card available for a holiday like President's Day or the Fourth of July, make your own card and send it. Your faraway relative will really feel appreciated.

Family Chain Letters

You may have a special group of relatives you enjoy hearing from often. One way to stay in touch is by writing family chain letters with them. Chain letters are a great way to keep families up-to-date on each other's lives until you meet again. It gives relatives a chance to receive regular mail from each other.

Here's how a family chain letter works:

1. Start by making a name and address list of the relatives who want to participate in the chain letter. Put yourself at the bottom. Make a copy of the list.

2. Write a letter to the first person on the list. Begin your letter something like this:

```
Dear Family,

This is the start of a family chain letter.
I'm also sending you a name and address list.
After you read this letter, please write your
own letter to the next person on the list.
Then send it to that person — along with this
letter and the list.
```

3. Continue your letter with news about yourself, your family, and other family members who live nearby. Then put your letter (and your copy of the list) in the mail.

4. As each person who receives the chain letter writes to the next person on the list, the stack of letters will grow. The last person on the list (that's YOU) will receive a lot of letters.

5. If you enjoyed the first family chain letter, start another one.

On-Line Conferences

If you and some of your faraway relatives have computers and modems, make arrangements to subscribe to the same on-line service, like CompuServe, America Online, or Prodigy. Use E-mail to arrange a special time to go on-line for a family conference. This is usually a lot less expensive than long-distance phone calls, and many relatives from many places can all "chat" at the same time.

You can also set up an on-line conference on the Internet. If you're not sure how to do this yourself, ask a friend or relative for help. Millions of people today use the Internet, probably including someone you know.

Think of how much fun it would be to have an on-line conference with all of your cousins at once—or to turn on your computer and find E-mail from your favorite uncle or cousin.

A Map of Your Family's World

Imagine that one of your grandfathers lives in New York and the other lives in Los Angeles. Your favorite aunt is going to school in London, and the cousin you like best will be in Brazil for two years. You're in Wisconsin, and sometimes you feel very far away from people you love. You may feel sad and lonely when you think about the miles between you.

Here's one way to cheer yourself up: Get a large map of the world and hang it on a wall in your room. Write to your relatives and ask them to send you pictures of themselves. Then pin or tape the pictures to your map. Every day, you'll see the faces of the people you miss most. Just seeing them may inspire you to write letters or send postcards. When they write back, you'll feel even better.

Families are families, no matter how extended they are, no matter how far away some relatives may travel or live. With your help, everyone can stay close—the way all families should be.

My Family's Pedigree Chart

A form to copy, fill out, and keep.

Make photocopies of the My Family's Pedigree Chart form on pages 100–101. (TIP: Use an enlarger so your copy has more space for writing.) Then fill it in with facts about you and your family. Here's how to fill in your chart.

1. Put information about yourself on the first branch of the chart, by number 1. Information about your brothers and sisters goes on this part of the chart, too.

2. Put information about your parents on the next branches. Each parent is a separate branch. Number them 2 and 3. Genealogists—people who do family research professionally—write the man's (father's) information by number 2 and the woman's (mother's) information by number 3. They list marriage information (date and place) under the man's name. But since this chart is for you and your family, you can list the information however you want.

3. Add information about your grandparents and great-grandparents. If you know your great-great-grandparents' names, add extra numbers and lines for them. Go back in time as far as you can.

My Family's Pedigree Chart

N = Name
B = Born
P = Place
M = Married
D = Died

N_____
B _____
P _____

N_____
B _____
P _____

② N_____
   B _____
   P _____
   M_____
   P _____
   D_____
   P _____

① N_____
   B _____
   P _____

N_____
B _____
P _____

③ N_____
   B _____
   P _____
   D_____
   P _____

N_____
B _____
P _____

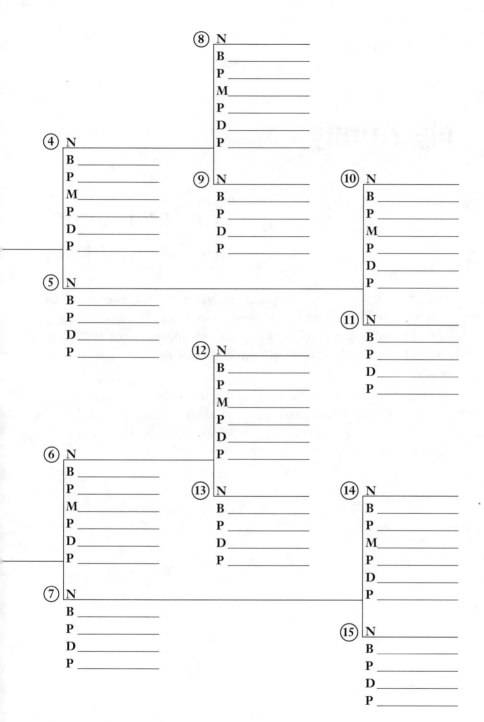

My Family

A form to copy, fill out, and keep.

HERE'S A FUN WAY to remember your family—and the things that are important to you and your family.

Make a photocopy of the My Family form on pages 103–104. Then fill it in with facts about you and your family. Paste in pictures.

Keep the completed form in your family history scrapbook, put it in your family time capsule, or include it in a family chain letter. Fill out a new copy of the form each year. See how your family is changing and growing.

My Family

Today's Date: _____

My Name _____

My Age _____

Dad's Name _____

Mom's Name _____

Sisters' Names _____

_____

_____

_____

Brothers' Names _____

_____

_____

_____

Names of Other Members of My Immediate Family

_____

_____

_____

Pets' Names _____

_____

_____

_____

Names of Favorite Relatives in My Extended Family

_____

_____

_____

_____

My Family

My Family's Favorite Restaurant _____

My Family's Favorite Holiday _____

The Things I Like Best about My Family _____

_____

_____

_____

_____

Our Favorite Place to Go Together _____

_____

_____

Our Favorite Thing to Do Together _____

_____

_____

Our Best Family Vacation _____

_____

_____

My Favorite Family Traditions _____

_____

_____

_____

_____

A Family Event I Remember Most _____

_____

_____

_____

_____

My Wishes, Dreams, and Hopes for My Family _____

_____

_____

_____

Index

A

Adopted families, 40-43, 51
Arguments, 24, 32

B

Bar Mitzvah/Bat Mitzvah, 84, 85
Big families. *See* Large families
Birthdays, 43, 85-86
Blended families, 1, 4-7. *See also*
    Stepfamilies
Boys Town National Hotline, 92
Buddhism, 22

C

Chain letters, family, 97
Chemotherapy, 47, *48*
Child Help National Child
    Abuse Hotline, 92
Chinese culture, 22-24
Christmas, 16-17, 84, 86, 87
Cinco de Mayo, 60
Collie dogs, 12-13, *12*
Crisis intervention, 92
Crises, families with, 47-50, *48*,
    49
Culturally different families, 40-
    43, *41*, *42*
Custody, parental, 8-10, *9*

D

Day of the Dead, 86
Disabilities in families, 18-21, *19*
Divorce, 1, 8-10, 22, 25-28
Down syndrome, 19, *19*, 20
Dysfunctional Families (Lynch), 92

E

E-mail, 67, 98
Easter, 87
Erlbach, Matthew, 64-65
*Everything You Need to Know About
    Family Violence* (Stark), 92
*Everything You Need to Know About
    Stepfamilies* (Glassman), 92

F

Families
    defined, 1
    extended, 93-98
    See also Relatives; types of
    families, e.g. Blended families
Family history, 62-74, 102-104
Family meetings, 90-92
    calling, 90
    conducting, 91
    outside help, 92
    voting, 11
Family problems, 92
Family standing, 13, 18

Poland, 56
Public libraries. *See* Libraries
Public records, and genealogy, 70

Q

Quilt, family, 77-78, *78*
Quinciñeras, 85

R

Racial differences, families with,
　33-36, *34*, *36*, 40
Ramadan, 87
Relatives, 93-98
　annoying, 95-96
　direct-line, 62
　families living with, 56-57, *57*
　families with distant, 22-24,
　23, 96-97
　families with nearby, 58-60,
　59, *60*
　spending time with, 94-95
　See also Family tree
Religion, families with differing,
　15-17, *16*, *17*
Respect, 25
Responsibilities, 11-14
Rosenberg, Maxine B., 92

S

St. Lucia's Day, 84
Same gender parents, 29-32, *30*
Scrapbooks
　birthday, 86
　family history, 73-74

Secret Santas, 87
Shadow box, family, 81-82, *81*
Sharing, 6, 52
Something's Wrong in My House
　(Leiner), 92
Stark, Evan, 92
Stepfamilies, 4-7, *5*, 44, *45*. *See
　also* Blended families

T

Television, 18
Thanksgiving, 86-87
Time capsule, family, 82-83
Timeline, family, 75-76, *76*
Traditions, family, 84-89
　birthday, 85-86
　holiday, 86-87
　personal, 87-88
　starting, 88-89
　types, 84-85
　See also Birthdays, Holidays
Twins, 30, 31

U

Unmarried parents, families
　with, 44-46

V

Voting, 11

Y

Youngest child. *See* Family
　standing

About the Author

Arlene Erlbach has written 32 books for young people—five young adult novels, four middle grade novels, and 23 nonfiction books. Her first book and first try at writing, *Does Your Nose Get In the Way, Too?*, won an RWA Golden Medallion. It was the lead book for the "Silhouette Crosswinds" line. A spin-off book, *Drop-Out Blues*, was a semifinalist the following year.

The Families Book is Arlene's second book for Free Spirit Publishing. Her first, *The Best Friends Book*, was published in 1995.

Arlene teaches students with learning differences at an elementary school, where she also directs the school's young authors program. She lives in Morton Grove, Illinois, with her husband, son, collie, and cats.

Clockwise from top: HERB (ARLENE'S HUSBAND), ARLENE (THE AUTHOR), SHERRY (THE COLLIE), MATTHEW (HERB AND ARLENE'S SON). *Not pictured:* ROBBIE, SPARKY, AND DUSTY, THE CATS.

About the Photographer

Stephen J. Carrera has been a Chicagoan since birth and has worked there with young people for more than 20 years. His involvement in urban youth-related programs includes peer counseling groups, gang crisis intervention, and teaching kids with behavior disorders and sixth graders. Presently he is disciplinarian and computer coordinator at a Chicago public school.

Photography has long been a passion for Stephen, who has done sports and news work for local newspapers as well as wildlife documentation and promotional pieces for conservation groups. His wife and two children enjoy accompanying him on excursions outside the city to hike and revel in nature's beauty, almost always documenting the experience through photographs.

More Free Spirit Books

The Best Friends Book: True Stories about Real Best Friends, Fun Things to Do with Your Best Friend, Solving Best Friends Problems, Long-Distance Best Friends, Finding New Friends, and More!
BY ARLENE ERLBACH
PHOTOGRAPHS BY STEPHEN J. CARRERA
This book blends stories from real-life best friends, pictures, and how-tos to celebrate friendship. It includes fun activities for friends to share, positive advice for making and keeping friends and dealing with problems friends sometimes face, and reproducible "Best Friend" forms for recording friendships in words and pictures. Ages 9-13.
$10.95; 96 pp.; B&W photos and illust.; s/c; 6" x 9"

The Best of Free Spirit®: Five Years of Award-Winning News & Views on Growing Up
BY THE FREE SPIRIT EDITORS
Hundreds of articles, tips, and cartoons on topics including "Self-Awareness and Self-Esteem," "Making a Difference," "Diversity," "Family and Friends," "Study Skills and Test-Taking Tips," and more. Everything is reproducible for home and classroom use. Ages 10 & up.
$24.95; 248 pp.; illust.; s/c; 8 1/2" x 11"

Laughing Together: Giggles and Grins from Around the Globe
BY BARBARA K. WALKER
Hundreds of jokes, riddles, rhymes, and short tales promote multiculturalism and global awareness through laughter, the universal language. Many are printed in their original language as well as English. For all ages.
$12.95; 132 pp.; illust.; s/c; 7 1/4" x 9 1/4"

The Young Person's Guide to Becoming a Writer
BY JANET E. GRANT
This comprehensive guide to starting and maintaining a writing career encourages young writers to discover their writing style, experiment with genres, evaluate their own work, and submit manuscripts for publication. It includes activities, tips, places to contact, recommended readings, and much more. Ages 12 & up.
$13.95; 184 pp.; s/c; 6" x 9"

Psychology for Kids: 40 Fun Tests That Help You Learn about Yourself
BY JONNI KINCHER
This creative, hands-on workbook promotes self-discovery, self-awareness, and self-esteem. Written by an educator, it is classroom-tested and based on sound psychological concepts. A Free Spirit best-seller! Ages 10 & up.
$14.95; 152 pp.; illust.; s/c; 8 1/2" x 11"

Psychology for Kids II: 40 Fun Experiments
That Help You Learn about Others
BY JONNI KINCHER
Based on science and sound psychological concepts and research, these experiments make it fun and interesting for kids to learn about their families, friends, and classmates. Includes 29 reproducible handout masters. Ages 12 & up.
$16.95; 168 pp.; illust.; s/c; 8 1/2" x 11"

Girls and Young Women Inventing: Twenty True Stories about Inventors
plus How You Can Be One Yourself
BY FRANCES A. KARNES, PH.D., AND SUZANNE M. BEAN, PH.D.
Not just for girls and young women, this book will inspire and motivate all young inventors. Includes real-life stories by successful young inventors, step-by-step instructions on how to be an inventor, up-to-date information about inventors' associations and organizations, a timeline of women inventors, and more.
Ages 11 & up.
$12.95; 176 pp.; B&W photos; s/c; 6" x 9"

The Kid's Guide to Service Projects: Over 500 Service Ideas
for Young People Who Want to Make a Difference
BY BARBARA A. LEWIS
The projects in this book range from simple things anyone can do to large scale commitments that involve whole communities. Readers can choose from a variety of topics including animals, crime, the environment, literacy, politics, and more. "Service Project How-Tos" offer step-by-step instructions for creating fliers, petitions, and press releases; fundraising; and more. Ages 10 & up.
$10.95; 184 pp.; s/c; 6" x 9"

School Power: Strategies for Succeeding in School
BY JEANNE SHAY SCHUMM, PH.D., AND MARGUERITE C. RADENCICH, PH.D.
This handbook for school success covers everything students need to know, from how to get organized to how to take notes, study smarter, write better, follow directions, handle homework, and more. Exciting graphics and straight-talk text make it appealing to kids; hundreds of how-to tips and techniques make it indispensable. Includes 17 reproducible handout masters. Ages 11 & up.
$11.95; 132 pp.; B&W photos and illust.; s/c; 8 1/2" x 11"

Stick Up for Yourself! Every Kid's Guide to Personal Power
and Positive Self-Esteem
BY GERSHEN KAUFMAN, PH.D., AND LEV RAPHAEL, PH.D.
Realistic, encouraging how-to advice for kids on being assertive, building relationships, becoming responsible, growing a "feelings vocabulary," making good choices, solving problems, setting goals, and more. Ages 8-12.
$8.95; 96 pp.; illust.; s/c; 6" x 9"

Also available:
A Teacher's Guide to Stick Up for Yourself
BY GERRI JOHNSON, GERSHEN KAUFMAN, PH.D., AND LEV RAPHAEL, PH.D.
$14.95; 128 pp.; s/c; 8 1/2" x 11"

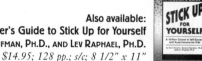

Find these books in your favorite bookstore, or write or call:
FREE SPIRIT PUBLISHING INC.
400 FIRST AVENUE NORTH, SUITE 616, MINNEAPOLIS, MN 55401-1730
TOLL-FREE (800) 735-7323, LOCAL (612) 338-2068
FAX (612) 337-5050
E-mail: help4kids@freespirit.com